RAILWAY WALKS
IN THE LAKE DISTRICT

© Peter Naldrett, 2015

All Rights Reserved. No part of this publication may be reproduced, stored in a retrieval system, or transmitted in any form or by any means – electronic, mechanical, photocopying, recording, or otherwise – without prior written permission from the publisher or a licence permitting restricted copying issued by the Copyright Licensing Agency, 90 Tottenham Court Road, London W1P 0LA. This book may not be lent, resold, hired out or otherwise disposed of by trade in any form of binding or cover other than that in which it is published, without the prior consent of the publisher.

Moral Rights: The author has asserted his moral right to be identified as the Author of this Work.

Published by Sigma Leisure – an imprint of Sigma Press, Stobart House, Pontyclerc, Penybanc Road, Ammanford, Carmarthenshire SA18 3HP.

British Library Cataloguing in Publication Data
A CIP record for this book is available from the British Library.

ISBN: 978-1-85058-991-4

Typesetting and Design by: Sigma Press, Ammanford.

Cover photograph: *Ratty* © Janice McGloine (see page 6 for further information)

Photographs: © Peter Naldrett unless stated otherwise.

Every effort has been made to fulfil requirements with regard to reproducing copyright material. The author and publisher will be glad to rectify any ommissions at the earliest opportunity

Maps: Sigma Press

Printed by: TJ International, Padstow, Cornwall

Disclaimer: the information in this book is given in good faith and is believed to be correct at the time of publication. No responsibility is accepted by either the author or publisher for errors or omissions, or for any loss or injury however caused. Only you can judge your own fitness, competence and experience. Do not rely solely on sketch maps for navigation: we strongly recommend the use of appropriate Ordnance Survey (or equivalent) maps.

RAILWAY WALKS IN THE LAKE DISTRICT

Peter Naldrett

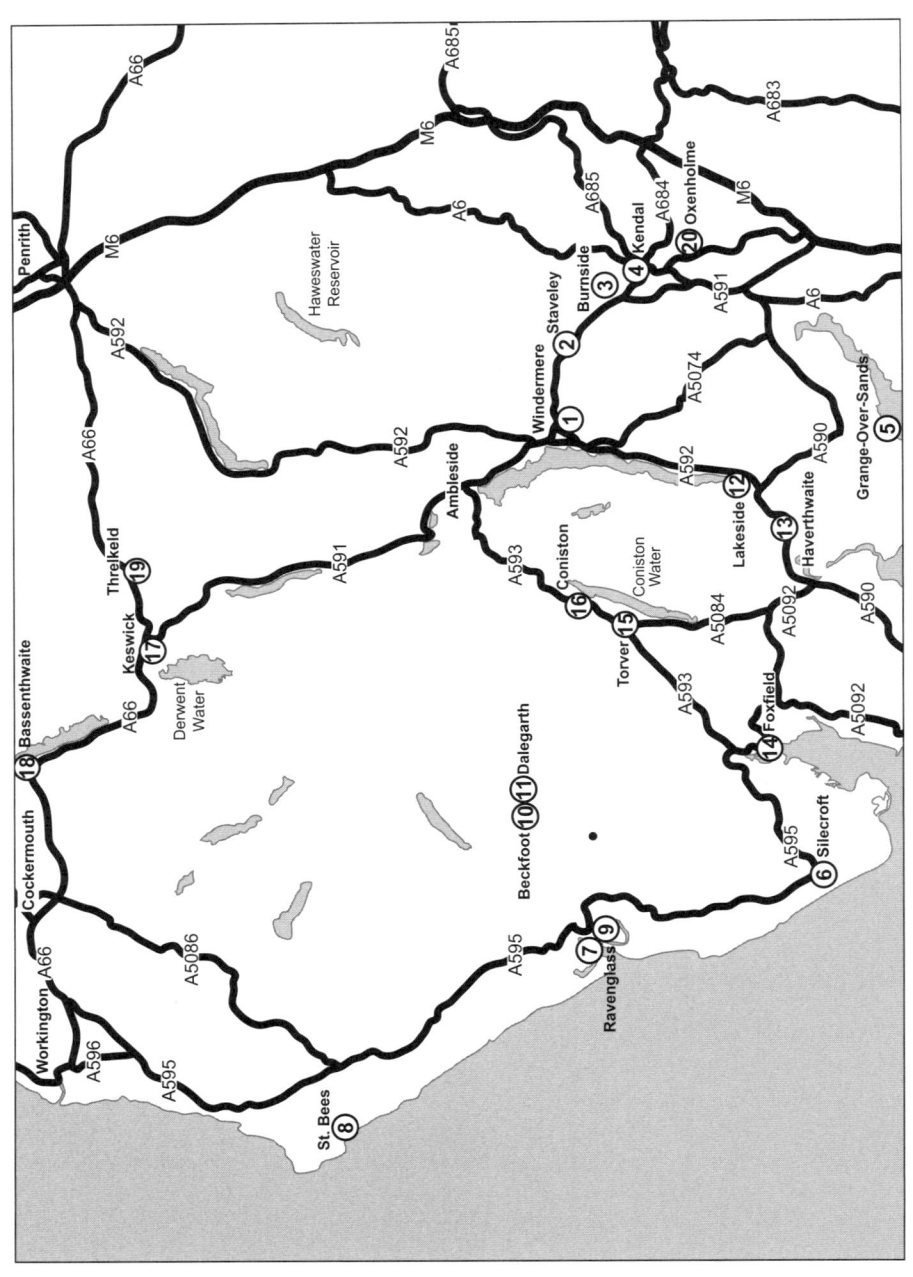

Contents

Introduction   7

TransPennine Route, Windermere Branch
1. Windermere   9
2. Staveley   14
3. Burnside   19
4. Kendal   25

Furness Line
5. Grange-over-Sands   31

Cumbrian Coast Line
6. Silecroft   39
7. Ravenglass   46
8. St Bees   52

Ravenglass and Eskdale Railway
9. Ravenglass to Irton Road   59
10. Beckfoot   64
11. Dalegarth for Boot   70

Lakeside and Haverthwaite
12. Lakeside   77
13. Haverthwaite   84

Coniston Line
14. Foxfield to Kirkby-in-Furness   91
15. Torver   96
16. Coniston   102

Cockermouth, Keswick and Penrith Railway
17. Keswick   108
18. Bassenthwaite Lake   113
19. Threlkeld   118

Main line
20. Oxenholme   123

This book is for Nicola, Toby, Willow and Neil.
Thanks for joining me on the walks.

Acknowledgement
Peter would like to thank Ben Brooksbank for kindly allowing the use of his photographs.

Janice McGloine

Lancashire born Janice is a self taught artist who has been painting professionally since 1993. She paints in her cosy studio and gallery which is at the Wolf House in Silverdale where she welcomes visitors to watch her at work on her latest piece.

She finds plenty of inspiration in this Area of Outstanding Natural Beauty. The ever changing coastline and unspoilt woodlands are constant revelation and her atmospheric land and seascapes reflect this.

She is fast becoming known for her "quirky" style paintings and prints of local villages and scenes. Her unique style and gentle colour palette is instantly recognisable and reflects the timeless quality of this beautiful part of the country.

Take a look at her website **www.janicemcgloine.com** or find her on facebook **www.facebook.com/jan.mcgloine**

INTRODUCTION

Whether it's rattling into Windermere, chugging out of Ravenglass or imagining how things used to be at Keswick Station, there is railway history to be found throughout the Lake District. As soon as the idea of rail travel started to take off, industrialists and tourists planned how it could be used in what is one of the most scenic regions in the country. In the Northern Lakes, bobbins helped Britain's booming Victorian textile factories, while in the south the quarries and mines benefited from powerful transport. As soon as the lines were built, they helped the working folk of Manchester and the rich tourists from the south of England gain access to the north-western beauties, arriving by the carriage load to experience the views from Windermere, the climbs from Keswick and the boat trips from Lakeside.

Some of Cumbria's lines have long since disappeared, cut away by the Beeching Axe in the 60s, while generally falling victim to overseas trade and the rise of the car. But there are plenty of train journeys still to be made in Cumbria and it's a great way to see the county. The main line to Glasgow has a special Lake District stop at Oxenholme, with connections taking you to Kendal and Windermere. Penrith, in the north, is still serviced by train. And it's possible to take the Cumbrian Coastal Line, a wonderfully remote route that takes in the seaside towns on the Lake District's fringe, taking its time to swing around the county's periphery over a series of viaducts and eventually reach Carlisle.

Nostalgia has also done wonderful things for Cumbria's railways. When the lines were first being constructed there was outrage from many locals who thought they would spoil the countryside – William Wordsworth among them. But we now look back at the age of steam through candy-rimmed glasses and we're keen to get aboard an old locomotive again, or at least see one whistling through the fields. Cumbria is now lucky to have a couple of heritage railways offering the chance for just that, with those based in Ravenglass and Haverthwaite feature in this book.

When you step out on the routes described here in Keswick, Threlkeld and others, you're stepping back in time, treading where the tracks were, pacing as passengers once did. Here, there's the opportunity to find out about the trains that used to operate and why they don't anymore. There are ruins to be found along the track, bridges that once carried freight and passengers, alongside station buildings now used for other purposes. And there's also a hope for the future as local groups continue to work tirelessly in order to relay the tracks to Keswick and bring a rail timetable to life once again.

When taken together, Cumbria has a wonderful railway tradition – past, present and future. These walks are designed to show you the best of the places and inform you about their past. Some you can visit by train still, others will need a car. But however you get there, I hope you have fun exploring the parts of Cumbria described in this book. The usual warnings should be taken heed of, including that you should always check the weather and take a map, sensible footwear, food, a GPS – and never solely rely on the descriptions and maps in the book, which are meant as a guide only. In a nutshell, take care, stay safe and have fun.

Peter Naldrett
www.peter-naldrett.co.uk   @peternaldrett
Member of The Outdoor Writers and Photographers Guild

WALK 1
Windermere

A circular walk from the train station up to Orrest Head, a hill with wonderful views of the lake.

Windermere Station

The original station opened in 1857 at the same time as the branch line from Kendal to Windermere. This is still a popular train station and it has seen passenger numbers increase over the last ten years to the current annual level of 359,000.

When it was built it was much larger than the current station, being home to four platforms and a roof over them. In 1973 the decision was made to save money and reduce the number of lines on the route from two to one, resulting in the current station being built. On the old site, the train sheds were demolished and the old station's façade and canopy were included in the design for the Booths supermarket which stands there today. Perhaps not obvious at first, but a quick glance at the side of Booths from the train station car park will give you a clue as to what the old station looked like and where it once stood.

Although the town surrounding the train station is now well known as 'Windermere' it wasn't going by that name before the railway arrived. The branch line terminated at a village called Birthwaite, with the station being named Windermere because that was the name of the nearby stretch of water. Over time, the name Windermere became associated with the settlement around the station, even though the waterside is actually 1km away. Nowadays, the name Windermere can apply to the water, the town and can even encapsulates nearby Bowness-on-Windermere which has grown and become linked to Windermere over the years.

The Kendal and Windermere Railway

The walks in this section of the book are based on the branch line that runs to Windermere from the west coast mainline, which was originally the Lancaster to Carlisle railway.

The engineer for the route was Joseph Locke, although he worked in partnership with others that included the father of steam travel,

Robert Stephenson. The branch line itself was not planned at the time of the Lancaster to Carlisle railway, but pressure for a line to Kendal grew when it was decided to take the route to Carlisle around the edge of the town. If the main line had called at Kendal it would have meant constructing a 3.5km tunnel a little further north, which proved to be too expensive. Instead, the main line was diverted around the east of Kendal and a branch line was then planned which left the main line at Oxenholme and went through Kendal en route to Windermere.

In the 21st Century it may seem rather quaint that rural settlements such as Staveley and Windermere have their own stations and survived the Beeching Axe in the 1960s. But back in the 19th Century when plans were being drawn up to bring steam engines into the Lake District, it was far from quaint and there was plenty of opposition – not least from poet William Wordsworth. He wrote a sonnet to the editor of the *Morning Star* which slammed the engineering intrusion, asking 'Is there no nook of English ground secure from rash assault?' A

Starting point	Windermere Railway Station car park (ND 414, 986)
Getting there	Windermere has a working train station. There are some direct trains from Manchester Airport and Preston, though you may find yourself changing at Oxenholme. Drivers should leave the M6 at Junction 36 and follow the A591 into Windermere, with the station being on the left as you enter the town
Length	3.4km / 2.1 miles
Allow	1 hr 15 mins
Refreshments	Stroll into the town of Windermere and you'll see The Queens on Victoria Street, which is a nice place to rest. Tel: 015394 43713 LA23 1AB www.thequeenswindermere.co.uk
Difficulty	Some steep climbs up to Orrest Head
Map	OS Explorer OL7 The English Lakes: South Eastern Area.
Nearest tourist information	Winderemere Tel: 015394 42895

Victorian case of Not In My Back Yard, perhaps. His objections, though, didn't stop the line going ahead and with permission being granted in 1845 the first trains rolled the full length of the track to Windermere in 1847.

At one time it was possible to get through trains to London from Windermere, which is no long the case. If you're heading to Manchester Airport, though, you're in luck.

Route

Start this walk by arriving at the Windermere Railway Station car park (grid reference ND 414, 986) and head for the main road. Turn right and go up the A591 on the pavement but after a short while keep an eye out for the path on the left through a gate and signed for Orrest Head and Common Wood.

Wander up this track, going through another gate on your way up. From here, pause to look behind you as Windermere is now in view, and the vision of it will become more stunning as you climb further. As you reach the top of the grassy bank you head through a gate and make your way into Common Wood, following the simple path through it.

When you do reach a junction of paths, go straight ahead following the sign once again for Orrest Head and Causeway Farm. You eventually reach a kissing gate and having gone through it you make your way over the wall to the left, following the path for Orrest Head. Climb up the final section of the hill up to Orrest Head, gradually seeing the trees thin out as you reach the summit.

Orrest Head is marked as having an outstanding view on the Ordnance Survey maps, and once you're there it's easy to see why. The far-reaching sight of Windermere and the patchwork of fells in the background are simply stunning.

Following the signs up to Orrest Head

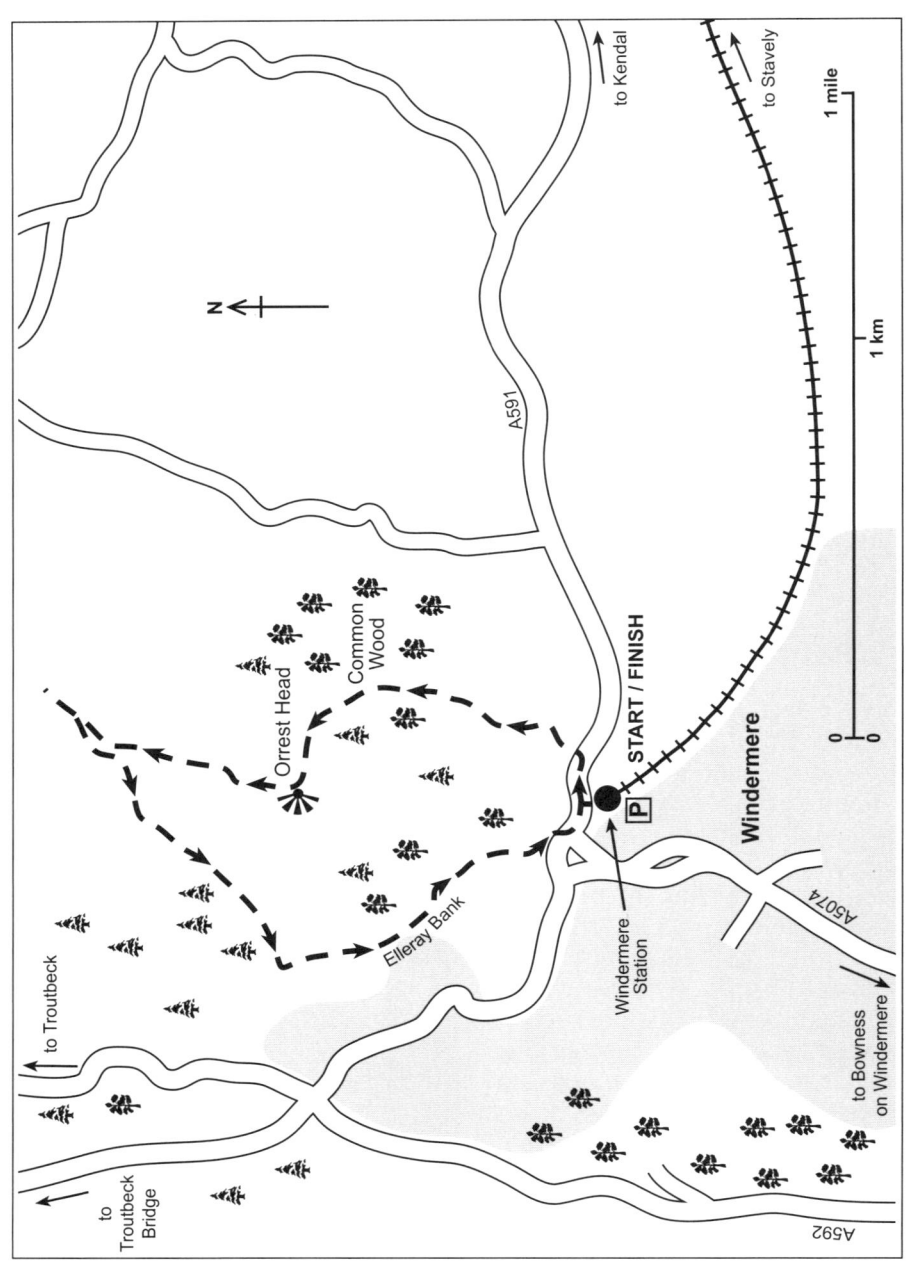

Orrest Head is a relatively simple climb, but the views give an accessible snapshot of what the Lakes has to offer

Once you've rested on the benches and taken in the scenery, make your way off the summit of Orrest Head, walking to the right (as you look at Windermere) and down the path. At the bottom of the hill, take the path straight ahead towards Causeway Farm, and this takes you some way across fields until you reach a junction of paths at SD 416, 999. Turn left here, slightly cutting back on yourself, and follow the path until you reach another junction, where you should turn left.

This route takes you by the side of High Hay Wood, and eventually into the trees until you reach a T-junction of paths at SD 404, 994. At this point, you need to turn left onto the track, following signs to Windermere. This path has the wood on the left and the backs of houses on the right, known as Elleray Bank. After a while, there will be a sign off to the left for Orrest Head, but you should head straight on towards Windermere. Soon, you will be brought out onto the main road and the railway station is across the road and up to the left.

WALK 2
Staveley

Close to Windermere but with a very remote character, Staveley is the key to accessing some of the lesser known fells and tarns in the Lake District.

Staveley Station
The final stop before Windermere on the branch line from Kendal, there is still a good and regular service to Staveley which may mean you want to head out for this walk on public transport. There's an hourly train going to Windermere during the week and some services will go straight through to Kendal from as far as Preston. Staveley used to be a request stop, but in late 2012 it became a mandatory stop, meaning that you don't have to worry about asking to get off here. There's only one platform at Staveley Station, used for travelling in both directions now that the branch has been reduced to one line. But back in the days when there were two railway lines heading through Staveley there used to be a second platform, which was located across the other side of the road near the now closed Railway Hotel.

Staveley
Not to be confused with Staveley-in-Cartmel which is also a village in southern Cumbria, Staveley near to Kendal is sometimes referred to as Staveley-in-Westmorland or, indeed, Staveley-in-Kendal. The population of the village grew in the late 19th century as a result of the railway passing through and providing a real boost to industry. It soon outgrew other, smaller settlements in the area and started to develop stronger links with Windermere and Burneside, which were the next stations along the line in each direction.

If you have some time to spare in Staveley before leaving, it's worth paying a visit to the Parish Church of St James, which was built in 1865 and boasts some impressive stained glass windows, including one showing the Ascension of Christ surrounded by angels. One of the angels on the window featured on a Royal Mail stamp at Christmas in 2009. Others may instead favour a visit to the Hawkshead Brewery on Mill Yard to sample a taste of some fine Lake District ale. Open from 9am to 5pm every day with a beer hall, it's worth checking their website to see if your trip will allow you to swing by to enjoy some Windermere Pale or Lakeland Gold.

Starting point	Stavely Train Station at grid reference SD 469, 980
Getting there	Take Junction 36 from the M6 and follow signs for Windermere on the A591. Once past Kendal, look out for a sign for Staveley's train station. You'll find street parking near the station, which marks the start of the walk (grid reference SD 469, 980). Getting here by train involves a change from the West Coast Mainline at Oxenholme The Lake District. Trains stop at Staveley on their way to Windermere
Length	9.7km/6 miles
Allow	2½ hours
Refreshments	Staveley is home to the Hawkshead Brewery at Mill Yard, where the Beer Hall is a great place to visit for some refreshment. www.hawksheadbrewery.co.uk Tel: 01539 822644 Postcode: LA8 9LR
Difficulty	Some steep sections up to Potter Tarn
Map	OS Explorer OL7 The English Lakes: South Eastern Area
Nearest tourist information	Kendal. Tel: 01539 735891
Next stations	Staveley is found in between the stations of Burneside and Windermere

Route

Staveley Railway Station is located near a T-junction of roads (grid reference SD 469, 980). To start, turn off the main road and go down the side road running parallel to the railway but then veering to the left. At the end of the road you will come to a river, where the road bends sharply to the right and leads to the main road through

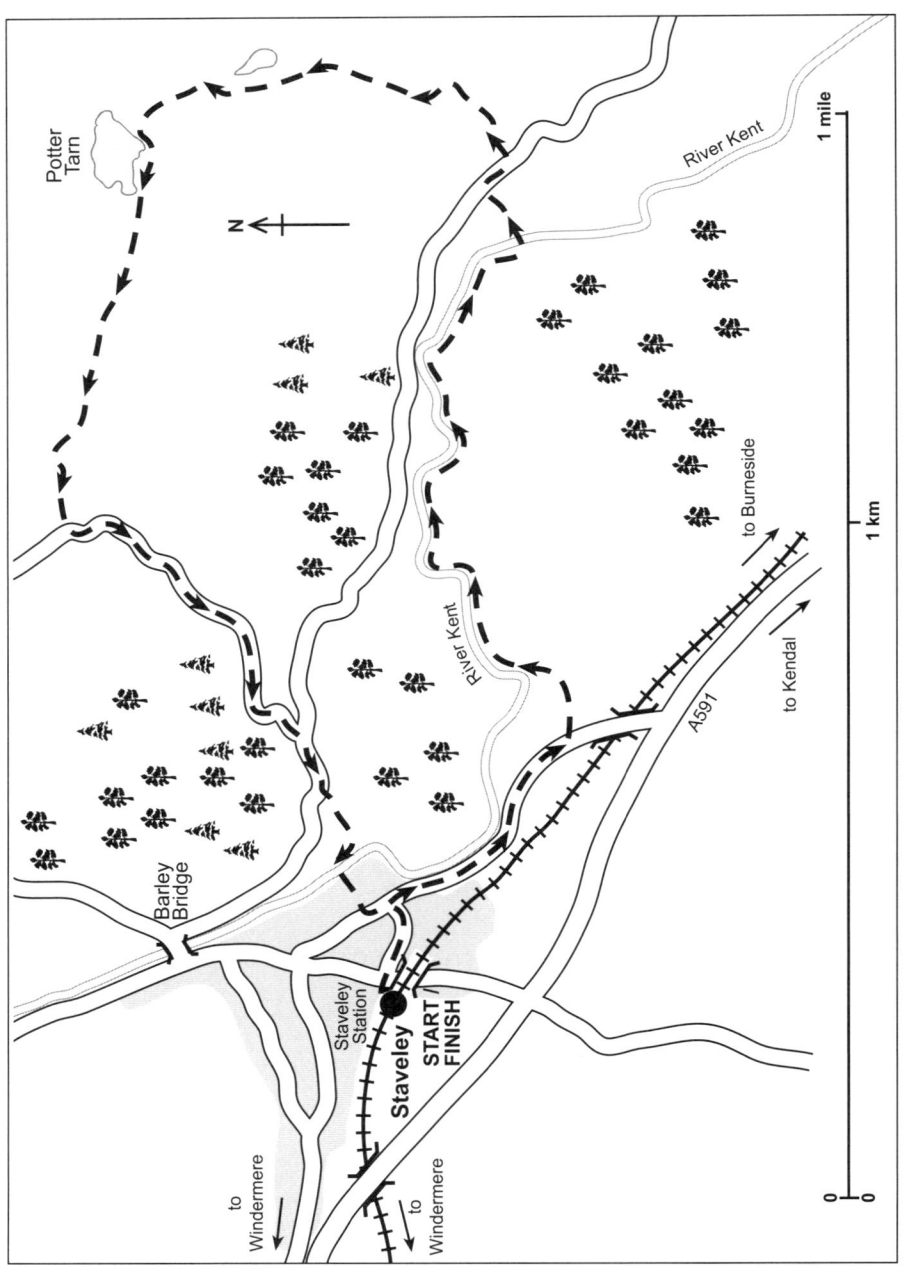

Staveley. Turn right onto the main road and walk on the left hand side of the road, with the River Kent on your left. As the main road leaves Staveley and bends slightly to the right, take the path across fields on the left which makes up part of the Dales Way. Soon after, follow the Dales Way as it branches off to the left and begins to stick close to the River Kent.

This is an easy route to follow on the right hand side of the river, and you don't turn off until you reach an obvious footpath at grid reference SD 491, 477. Cross over the river and head straight on at the other side, climbing up a hill before heading to the left side of the house at the top and reaching a road. Turn right on the road and walk for about 150 metres before taking the track on the left. Following this will bring you to a junction of paths at SD 496, 979, where you should turn left and follow the signs for Potter Tarn.

You're now heading onto the fells and sticking to a well-marked and

The stroll over fields on the way to Potter Tarn

easy to follow path up to Potter Tarn. As you climb, the views around and behind you get better and better. On your left you'll soon come to Ghyll Pool and then you've a similar distance again before you get to Potter Tarn, where you'll reach a junction of paths and should turn left (SD 494, 988).

Follow the path over the hill as it edges over a peak and starts to head down. Continue heading straight ahead and ignore two paths that turn off to the left. You'll eventually come to a sharp left turn that will take you by buildings at Birk Field and then up a slight incline to a road (SD 482, 990). Turn left onto the road and stick to this country track as it takes you down the hill.

When you reach Craggy Plantation on the right, you'll notice that the decline gets sharper and you enter a left bend followed by one to the right. Coming to a junction of roads, turn right and look out for a path on the left soon after. This takes you across a couple of fields, beyond some houses and eventually to the River Kent, where you need to turn right and cross over the footbridge.

At the other side of the river, continue straight ahead on the road, turning left when you meet the main road through Staveley. Look out for a church on the left and soon after take the footbridge on the right which takes you over another stream. At the other side of this one, take a right turn and follow the road back to the starting point.

WALK 3
Burneside

Frequently overlooked by tourists heading deeper into the Lakes, Burneside provides an unlikely place for a lovely walk by the River Kent along the Dales Way and over farmland.

Burneside

Sitting just outside the National Park, the village surprises walkers at first as it is quite industrial. Although a number of mills originally sat on this stretch of the River Kent, today the primary employer of the area is the remaining paper mill at Burneside, James Cropper. Initially it seems out of place on the boundary of the Lake District, but the mill is an important employer and once you have walked around the site it is easy to forget that it's there. Elsewhere, the village plays host to a chip shop and a pub called Jolly Anglers, though there is not as much to occupy your time as in nearby Staveley. Worth looking out for, though, is the large church of St Oswalds, rebuilt in the 1880s and dominating the main street of the village.

Blast from the past: Going back to the days when there were two tracks on the line

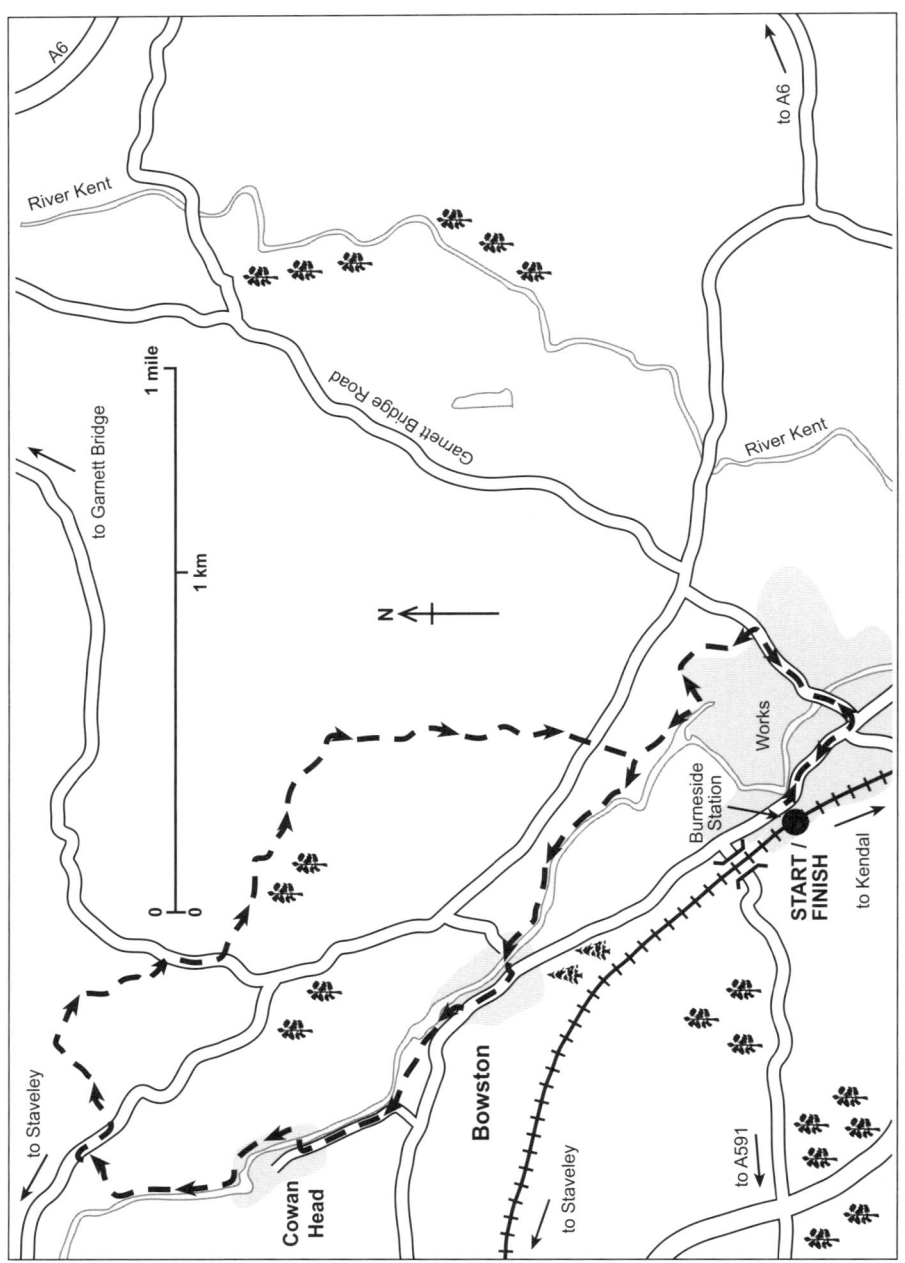

The train station, which was a request-only stop until late 2012, has become more and more important to the village over the last decade and passenger numbers have doubled. Direct services run from here to Windermere, Manchester and Preston providing a link that many rural communities can only dream of.

Starting point	Burneside Train Station: SD 502, 957
Getting there	Burneside is easily reached from Junction 36 of the M6, following signs for Windermere and then looking for the Burneside turning on the right
Length	5.5km / 3.4 miles
Allow	1½ hours
Refreshments	Jolly Anglers Tel: 01539 732552 Postcode: LA9 6QS
Difficulty	Some brief, steep climbs halfway through the walk, elsewhere mainly flat
Map	OS Explorer OL7 The English Lakes South Eastern Area
Nearest tourist information	Kendal. Tel: 01539 735891
Next stations	Back towards the West Coast Mainline you'll come to Kendal, while heading out towards Windermere the next station is Staveley

Route

Burneside Station is well signposted from the A591 road and is found at grid reference SD 502, 957. From this small station, head down to the main road that runs through Burneside and turn right. You walk past the impressive church and a pub called Jolly Anglers before turning left on the road to Skelsmergh.

Continue on this road until you see a roadside path up on the left signed for the Dales Way and then shortly after take the path to the left, heading for Bowston. This is the Dales Way and the first bit of the path is fenced in and takes you around the James Cropper building. Once you're clear of the paper mill, you enter fields and

The first section of the walk takes you by the River Kent

continue along the Dales Way at the side of the River Kent. There's a weir on your left at this point and there's an instant change in atmosphere once you leave the pocket of industry behind.

In the first field, there's no need to go up the hill. Just stick to the left hand side and follow the fence around, then head over the wall and into the next field. There's soon another stile to go over as you make your way through the fields, keeping the river on your left.

This path takes you into the small settlement of Bowston, and you reach it by heading up the steps from the field and onto the road. Turn left into Bowston and when you reach the first junction turn right. Walk along the road for a while and before long you'll see the path you need on the right, which is the Dales Way heading for Staveley.

The River Kent is now on your right. You pass another weir and soon come onto a private road, turning right onto it. This takes you into Cowan Head, where you keep to the left of the old mill building that is now converted into apartments, and then go between the rows of white cottages. The Dales Way continues through a gate, with the river once more next to you on the right. Keep on this path until you reach a footbridge, at grid reference SD 491, 977, where you cross over the River Kent. Go through the gate, climb up the track, go beyond the farm house to the road and turn right onto it. Shortly after, take the bridleway off to the left and climb up, beyond gates and sticking the track with walls on either side of you. At grid reference SD 496, 979, go through the gate and take the bridleway heading down to the right, signed for Mirefoot.

Stick to this main track, heading beyond Mirefoot cottages until you reach the road, where you then turn right. Shortly after, look out for a bridleway on the left and take that, continuing ahead with a wall on the right and a hedge on the left. This takes you up to Braban House, with the path going round the back of the building and you'll come to a junction of paths.

Take the bridleway to the right and then before long you'll see the path you need off to the left. This takes you across a field, where you go over the brow of the hill and aim for the far left side, where you turn left and go over a little stream using stepping stones. Turn right here and continue on the path, which keeps to the right hand side of the fields, sticking close to the fences and walls there. This will bring you out at a road, which you need to cross and pick up the path at the other side heading to Burneside.

When you reach the bridge, turn left and continue along the path as it goes by the paper mill. You're now retracing your steps from the first section of the walk, so turn right when you reach the road and then right onto the main road. This will take you back to the train station, on the left.

The Dales Way

Despite heading through the Lake District and Peak District National Parks, The Dales Way is not one of the most challenging long distance paths in the country. Covering some 84 miles between Windermere and Ilkley, the highest point on the trek is 490 metres above sea level at Cam Houses. Although the climb and descent at that point is steep, the Dales Way does actually avoid some of the larger hills. Instead, the walk gives you a treat by sticking to the scenic valleys of rivers such as the Kent, Dent, Mint and Wharfe.

A week should be a comfortable time to complete this walk, and it's a great one to plan out because of the facilities on the route. There

New apartments give residents a lovely view down onto the River Kent

are train stations close to the start and finish, while many of the pubs along the way do bed and breakfast. And you'll be going through some great places as well, seeing the landscape change from the rolling dales of West Yorkshire to the distinctly different fells of the Lakes. Dent, Grassington, Kettlewell, Sedbergh, Burneside and Staveley are all on the route, with Kendal close by as well.

WALK 4
Kendal

There is plenty to see and do in this Lakeland town, which prides itself as being the 'gateway' to the fells. Although more 'urban' than other walks in this book, it's great to explore the river and castle close by Kendal's train station.

Kendal Castle
The walk passes by the site of Kendal's castle, a place rich in history that dates back to the 12th century. The building today is a ruin, a mass of slowly crumbling stone that hints of its glory days when noble men and women gazed at the same view you enjoy today. Well, almost

I'm still standing: the remains of Kendal Castle

the same view. The M6 wasn't there back in Henry VIII's day and Kendal was a lot smaller. But you get my point. This, however, was not Kendal's first castle. A motte castle was built across on the other side of town around 1087, but it was abandoned by the 13th century, at which time Kendal Castle was becoming well established. Kendal Castle was first built by the de Lancaster family, who were barons of

Starting point	Kendal Train Station at grid reference SD 519, 932
Getting there	Kendal is easy to reach from the M6 motorway, not far from Junction 36. Follow the signs for the town and you'll soon be there, with the train station being signed once you are in the centre. If you're heading on the train, you may have to change at Oxenholme The Lake District. Trains to Kendal are frequent and it's a good base for a public transport -based walk
Length	3.1km / 1.9miles
Allow	1 hour
Refreshments	There are many pubs to choose from in Kendal, and you'll no doubt see some if you deviate from the route to check out the town's shops. You may come across Burgundys on Lowther Street Tel: 01539 733803 LA9 4DH www.burgundyswinebar.co.uk and there's also The Shakespeare Inn on Highgate. Tel: 01539 724069 LA9 4HE
Difficulty	There is a fairly steep hill to climb halfway on your way to the castle. All else is straightforward, with several town centre roads
Map	OS Explorer OL7 The English Lakes South Eastern Area
Nearest tourist information	Kendal, 25 Stramongate, Kendal, LA9 4BH Tel: 01539 735891
Next stations	Access to Kendal by train is gained from Oxenholme, changing from the West Coast Mainline. Coming from Windermere, Kendal is the stop after Burneside

Kendal, and they chose to construct it from earth and timber. It was rebuilt using stone at the end of the 12th century and passed hands several times, with the Crown owning it for a while and Richard II giving it to the Parr family, the one that later produced Catherine Parr who married Henry VIII.

Sadly for historians, some of the stone has been carried away to be used on other buildings down the years and it is not clear what all sections of the castle were used for. However, it is possible to make out the private apartments, the large hall and the kitchens.

Route

Walking down the main exit from the train station, you'll come to a junction of roads with a roundabout. From here, head over to the left towards Ann Street, which is a terraced road with a shop on either corner. Continue down Ann Street until you come to Castle Street at the end, where you should turn left.

Heading along Castle Street, look out for Castle Road which you'll spot just before you come to the railway bridge overhead. Go along Castle Road and as it bends off to the left you need to take the path

The centre of Kendal

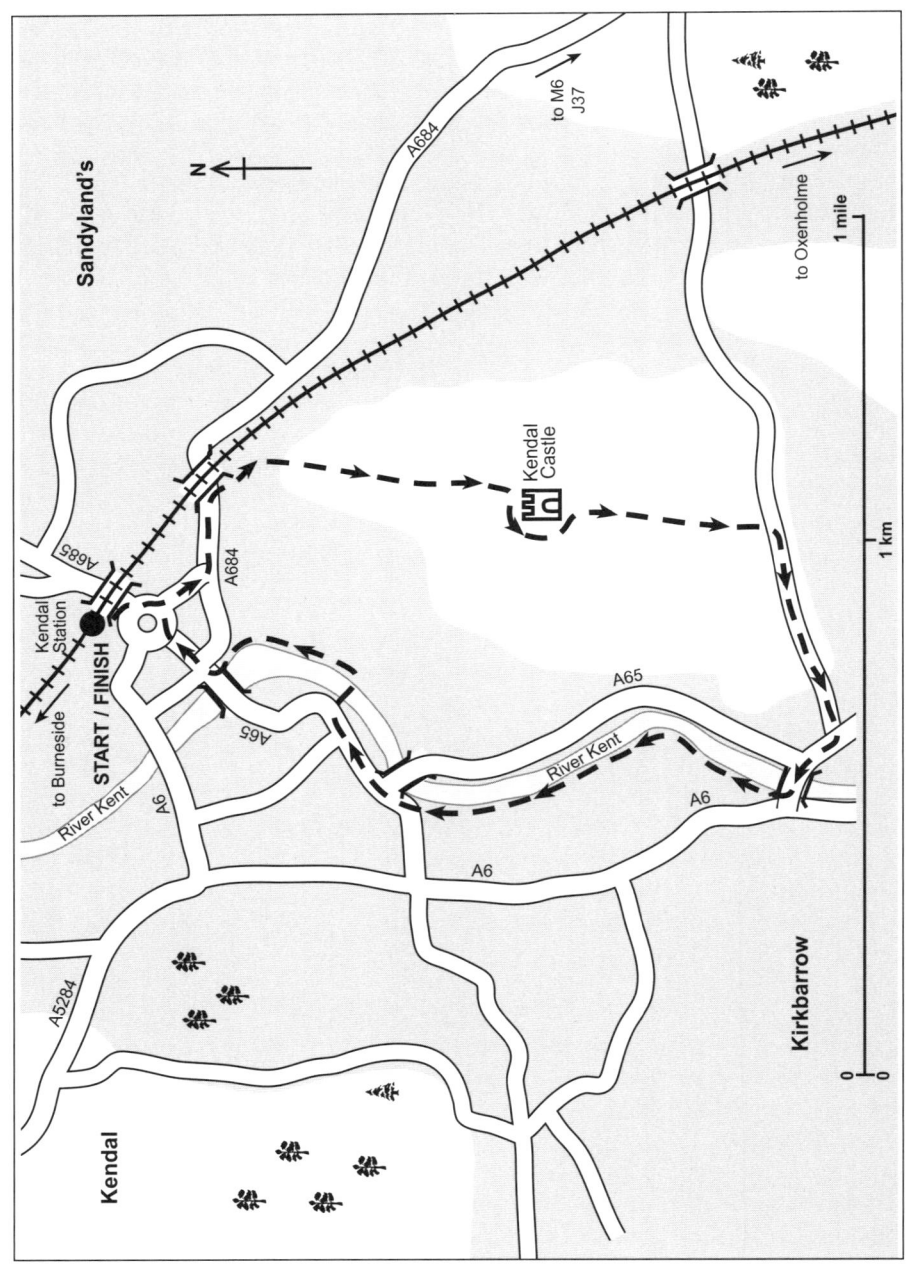

As you walking alongside the River Kent, you'll see the charming Parish Church in the centre of Kendal

off to the right, clearly signed for Kendal Castle. This takes you up a grassy mound, where great views of the town and surrounding Lakeland begin to appear. Up and up this goes, on a short but steep climb to the ruins of the castle.

When you get to the castle site, have a good explore of the ruins and wander around the old walls. But when you're done, head directly to the opposite side to that you climbed up on, taking the continuation of this path down the slope at the other end. The path heads straight down the hill, passing a few trees and then continuing ahead through a cemetery.

You'll eventually come out at Park Side Road, where you should turn right. Continue right to the end of the road, where you will come to a junction with Lound Road. Turn right here and follow it to the left as Lound Road adopts the bridge over the River Kent. When you get across the river, follow a sign for the Parish Church. At the end of the bridge, turn right again and keep an eye out for the path you'll need on the right which takes you by the side of the river once again. Along this well used and well established path, you'll soon see a church on your left.

Continue ahead along this charming riverside walk, eventually passing a café before you make your way up to the road. Turn right here, following the A6 'New Road' as it bends to the right. You need to stick to the right hand side of the road and head through the car park until you see a green footbridge over the river on your right. Cross the river here, and turn left at the other side on the path through Gooseholme Park. When you get to the end of the path, turn right onto Castle Street and then look for Ann Street on your left. At the end of Ann Street you will be able to see Kendal Train Station across the road.

WALK 5
Grange-over-Sands

From just above sea level at Grange's train station, climb to one of the finest fell-top views of the southern Lakes.

Grange-over-Sands Station

The original station still stands to preside over the comings and goings on the historic Grange-over-Sands platforms. The line opened in 1857, but it was not until the mid-1860s that the station was built by Lancaster architect E.G. Paley, who also designed several other train stations for the Furness Railway Company.

First built with the purpose of gaining faster access to iron ore materials, it was soon obvious that Grange could benefit from the passenger trains bringing early tourists from industrial Lancashire towns and it's from here that the resort started to develop. The station

Welcome to Grange! The station here has remained largely unchanged since it was opened *(photograph: Ben Brooksbank)*

is still a stunning sight, with its ornate shelters providing respite from the Cumbrian weather, not least because it received a full make-over in the late 1990s to restore it to its former glory. Originally named simply 'Grange', it was renamed 'Grange-over-Sands' by Furness Railway in 1916 and that's the way it has stayed ever since. Today, the trains that call at the station are run by Northern Rail and First TransPennine Express.

Grange-over-Sands

Grange-over-Sands itself developed in Victorian Days as a popular tourist destination, with

The ornate decoration makes this a stand-out Victorian station

the railway line aiding people from cities such as Manchester and Liverpool to escape to the picturesque resort between the sea and the mountains. Standing on the mile-long promenade that is a key feature of Grange's geography, it's easy to see why the 'over-Sands' was added to the name. The town is, quite literally, on the edge of the vast expanse of sand that Morecambe Bay keeps revealing when the tides allow.

When Victorian visitors arrived on the trains to take some of the healing sea air, they stood on the same promenade and looked upon the River Kent sweeping by the sea wall. Today, as you'll see, the River Kent has shifted its position over the 20th century and now a grassy area can be found at the bottom of the sea wall as you look across the bay. Look at the OS map and you'll see a footpath heading straight across the bay, a throw-back to the days before the trains when tradesmen made the treacherous journey on foot over the sand. But you MUST NOT head out onto the sands as they can be extremely dangerous – as demonstrated by the 2004 tragedy in which 23 Chinese cockle pickers died before they could escape the racing tide.

The dangers were known so early on that since the 16th century there has been a Royal Guide to take control of making sure intrepid travellers get across the bay safely. Trips across with the current guide can be taken in the summer months, usually as part of a charity event, and you should contact the local tourist office for more information.

Hampsfield Fell
At the southern tip of the National Park, this fell has been immortalised in Wainwright's books and is generally considered to

Starting point	The train station at Grange-over-Sands, grid reference SD 411, 781
Getting there	Leave the M6 motorway at Junction 36, heading for Kendal. After a couple of miles, take the A590 signed for Grange over Sands. Follow the signs for the town and then the train station. The train station car park is for rail users only. There is limited car parking on the road outside the station, or a nearby council car park. This is a working station and you are also able to catch a train here to start the walk
Length	4.7km / 2.9miles
Terrain	1¾ hours
Refreshments	If you've come on the train, a short walk into the centre of Grange from the train station will introduce you to many places to get refreshments. Those in the car may fancy the short drive to Allithwaite for a visit to The Pheasant Inn. www.thepheasantinnallithwaite.co.uk 015395 32239. LA11 7RQ
Difficulty	Some steep climbs at first, as well as roadside walking and some rocky terrain
Map	OS Explorer OL7 The English Lakes South Eastern Area
Nearest tourist information	Grange-over-Sands Tel: 015395 34026
Next stations	Back on the line towards Manchester the next station is Arnside, while Kents Bank is in the direction of Barrow

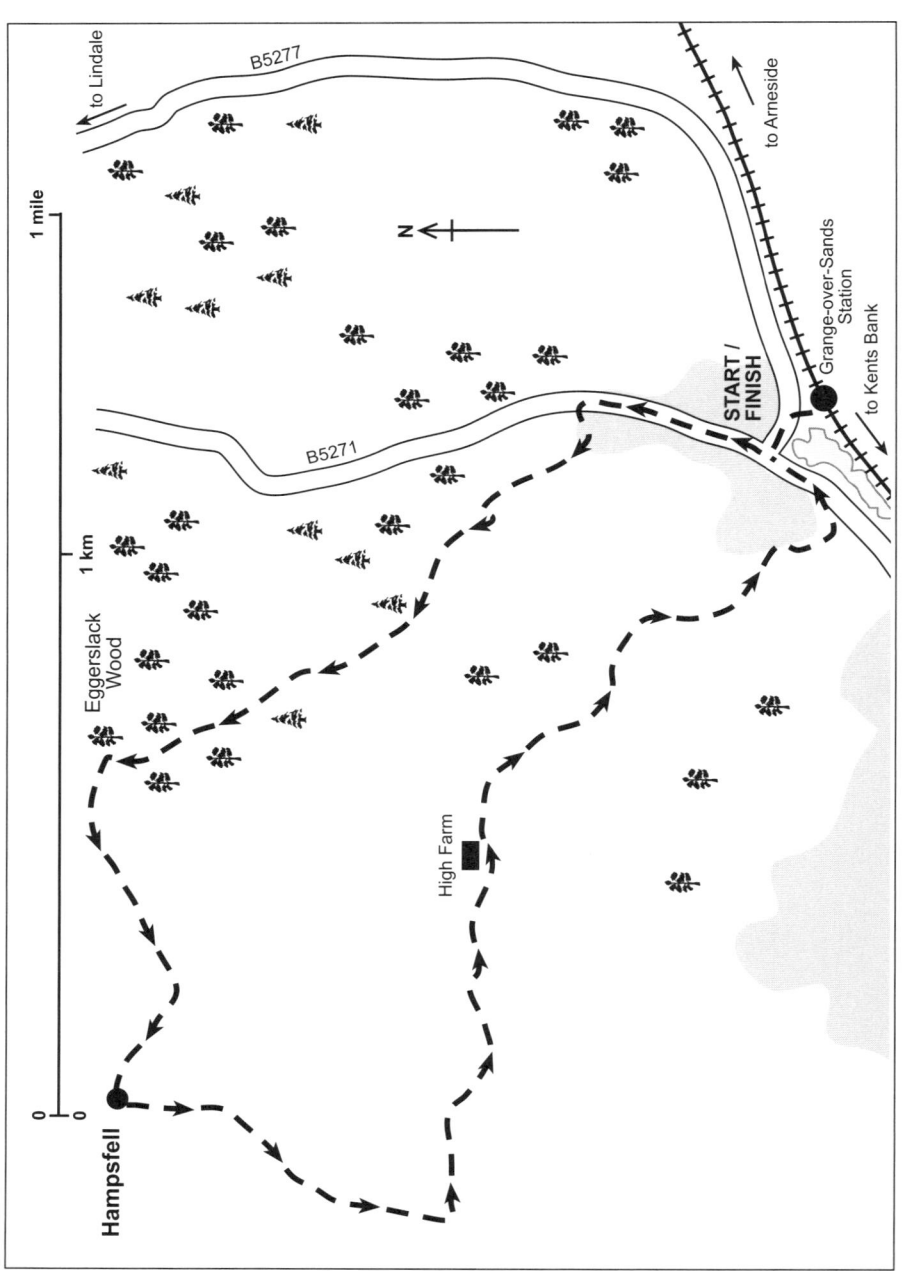

give the most magnificent views of the fells as they gently make way for Morecambe Bay. Reaching a height of 222 metres above sea level, it might not be considered one of the highest mountains in the Lake District, but when you consider that you're pretty much starting at sea level it can be a tough ascent. Generally called Hampsfell, a shortened and more popular title, there is more to welcome you at the top than the astounding views. Hampsfell Hospice , as it's known, stands proudly at the top, a limestone shelter which can keep you out of the changeable Cumbria weather but also serve the dual purpose of informing you about surrounding hills.

Route

From the train station at Grange-over-Sands (SD 411, 781), head for the main road and turn left. When you reach the roundabout after a few metres, turn right and follow the road sign for Windermere. Carry on walking beyond the houses on the path at the side of the road. Shortly after the road bends to the left, there is a path off to the left which you take, signed for Hampsfell.

The wide expanse of Morecambe Bay affords some fantastic views and even better sunsets

Caption here

Head up through a wood and when you come to a track crossing in front of you, head straight across, taking the path up the hill once more. Carry on up the hill along what is becoming a steep section of the walk and you'll also notice the start of some limestone rocks on the ground, the prevalence of which will become greater as you climb. Soon you'll come to another path which crosses your route and this time you need to head across once more and take the path which heads up to the left, this one being well signed for Hampsfell.

You're now in the middle of Eggerslack Wood, and you should keep ahead on the path which is easy to follow and well signed by markers. When you come to an old wall on the right, you'll see a junction of paths and you should carry on up the hill straight ahead of you, where the limestone outcrops appear again.

Eventually, after heading through the wood for some time, you will come to a clearing and a dry stone wall marking the boundary between the wood and the fell. There is a stile over the wall, which you need to climb over. Once over, follow the sign leading you onto the path in front of you, marked for the Hospice. You'll soon be up amongst the bracken on the fells, with more and more limestone helping to make this a really spectacular environment.

Markers send you higher on up the hill and pretty much straight away at this stage of the walk you can stop to have a look at the ever-increasingly beautiful view behind you, beyond the woods. You'll be able to get a wonderful perspective of Morecambe Bay and the southern fells of the Lake District.

As you reach a brow in the hill, you'll come to a limestone wall, which you go over. Turn right onto the path afterwards and follow it up next to the wall. This will bring you out at the top, to the Hospice, which is a great place to shelter and take in the view. From the summit, follow the path which leads away from the Hospice to the left (as you approached it) and takes you down towards Morecambe Bay. The views here on a fine day are great, taking in all the settlements on the bay itself, the Ashton Memorial at Lancaster, the power station at Heysham and even Blackpool Tower.

Keep heading down and you'll eventually come to a wall, where you head over a stile and go straight on. At grid reference SD 397, 789 you'll see a marker where the paths split in two, and you need to take the one on your left here. At the next junction of paths, turn left and head down the hill with Morecambe Bay now sitting nicely in front of you. You'll see a series of square fields in front of you and you should head for the wooden gate, go over the wall and head across the field, going through another gate before you reach the end. Through a gate at the other side, the path then goes diagonally across the next field and brings you to a farm track, where you need to turn left.

Go past High Farm and you'll eventually reach a junction of paths, with the one you're needing bending round to the right, signed for Grange-over-Sands. Follow this road right down the hill until you pass a large white house on the right and, at grid reference SD 407, 781, you see a path for Grange on the left. Take this and it brings you out onto a road, which you follow and then turn right down the hill to the main road. Turn left onto the main road and right at the roundabout to reach the train station where the walk started.

WALK 6
Silecroft

A small request stop on the Cumbria Coast route, Silecroft is well worth investigating because of its beautiful and quiet stretch of beach set against the backdrop of the fells.

The Cumbria Coast Line

From Barrow-in-Furness, in the south, right the way up to Carlise, this link track which skirts the western and northern edges of the Lake District is known as the Cumbria Coast Line. It completes the loop which starts with the Furness Line from Carnforth via Grange-Over-Sands and Ulverston and provides a vital link for small and rather remote villages and towns. The coastal line gives access to the West Coast Mainline, and so to London and Glasgow.

Of course, when the railways were being built in the 19th century there were private companies all competing with different routes. The Cumbria Coast Line is a fine example of a line which has developed in a piecemeal fashion, although there are little signs to remind you of

Silecroft Station in the 1960s *(photograph: Ben Brooksbank)*

this today. The first section of track to be built saw the Furness Line from Barrow-in-Furness to Kirkby-in-Furness extended and opened in 1844. One year later, at the northern end of the Lake District, the line from Carlisle to Maryport was developed and opened up as the Carlisle and Maryport Railway. The completion of the full loop from Carnforth to Carlisle, however, took another two developments in the middle, the first being the Whitehaven and Furness Railway which built the lengthy stretch from Whitehaven to Kirkby-in-Furness. The

A short stroll from the station brings you to a wide expanse of beach

Whitehaven Junction Railway oversaw the development of the route from Whitehaven to Maryport. All these sections eventually became united under one operator in 1923 when the London, Midland and Scottish Railway acquired the length of the track.

Nowadays the services are run by Northern Rail, linking the 26 stations on the route and some direct trains heading further south to Lancaster and Preston. In 2008, the Cumbria Coast Line was designated a Community Rail Line to signify the close links with local people and businesses and, one year later, the train service was adapted to alleviate the impacts of the floods which hit this part of Cumbria. An extra service was put on every hour between Maryport and Workington, while a temporary station was in place at Workington North until 2010.

Starting point	Silecroft Train Station, just off the A5093, at grid reference SD 130, 819
Getting there	The train from Barrow-in-Furness will take around 33 minutes to reach Silecroft, while from Carlisle you are looking at a 1hr 50 min journey if you get a direct train. By car, Silecroft is reached by taking the A595 from Junction 36 of the M6, following it round to the Cumbrian coast
Length	6.1km / 3.8 miles
Terrain	1¾ hours
Refreshments	King William IV is found at Kirkstanton, near enough to call in after the walk if you're in the car. If not, the walk passes close to Kirkstanton so check on the map if you want to make a detour
Difficulty	An easy circular walk that will cause few problems
Map	OS Explorer OL6 The English Lakes South Western Area
Nearest tourist information	Broughton. Tel: 01229 716115
	Next stop heading north is Bootle, and if you're venturing south you'll come to Millom

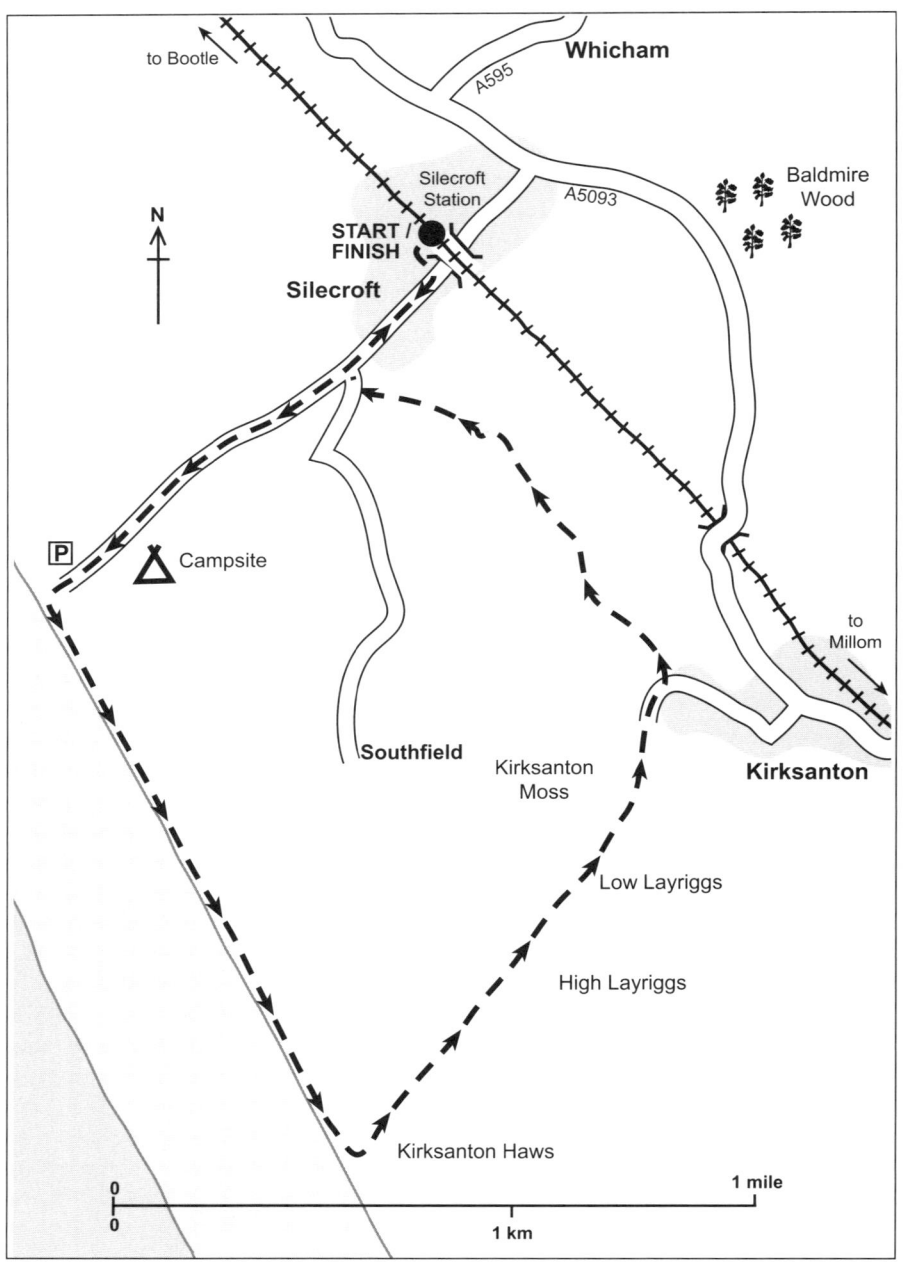

Today, the only branching passenger line to run off from one of the line's stations is the narrow gauge tourist route from Ravenglass – walks from which can be found in this book. But at one time there were plenty of branch lines leaving this coastal route, including those to Silloth, Coniston and Cockermouth. Silloth and Cockermouth became victims on the Beeching Axe in the mid 1960s, and today we're left to ponder how these places would have developed differently if trains had continued to rattle into their centres.

Route

If you're arriving for this circular walk by train the route starts at the railway station but if you're coming by car there is limited parking around the station so probably best to head for the car park at the end of the road heading to the coast (grid reference SD 121, 811).

From the train station, head for the road which heads through Silecroft and turn right onto it, heading out towards the sea. This generally quiet road continues ahead, taking you past a camping and caravan site on the left before bringing you out at the coast, where the stunning environment includes a wonderful stretch of sand and pebbles, an offshore wind farm and, on a clear day, the hilly outline of the Isle of Man.

You're now at the car park and those coming by car may find it easier to start from here. When you reach the beach, head onto it and turn left so that you are walking straight ahead with the sea on your right. This is a wonderful way to pass time and the stretch along the sand is the highlight of this round walk. The top of the beach is covered with pebbles and, as such, can prove tricky to walk on so if the tide allows it's better to stride out on the sand.

Keep an eye out for the triangulation pillar on the left, part of a network of over 6000 that helped Ordnance Survey map the country. Normally found atop hills and mountains, this is one of the lowest in the country, clocked at 16 metres above sea level. You'll also be able to see the wind farm ahead of you, in fields on the left. Before you reach the huge turbines, though, look for a track on the left (grid reference SD 128, 796).

This farming track is easy to follow as it takes you beyond High Layriggs and Low Layriggs before coming onto a road. When there is a sharp turn to the right, the walk follows a footpath that heads off to the left – although if you fancy a detour to the pub in Kirkstanton

This interesting round walk takes you by the sea, within sight of large fells and across coastal farmland

you need to follow the road around to the right. The path that you're following is on a good track heading to Standing Stones Farm and when you reach the farm you need to follow the path into a field on the right. There is a choice of two paths to take here and you take the one on the left. Follow the path as it shadows a waterway and then cross over via a footbridge before continuing ahead on the path through fields.

The path eventually turns into a track and will bring you out at a small country road, where you turn right and head towards a T-junction. Turn left here (SD 128, 816) and head along the road to the car park if that's where you started from. If you began at the railway station, you will need to turn right here and look for the station on your left.

Silecroft

Serving a small community on the Cumbrian Coast line between Barrow-in-Furness and Carlisle, there are no evening services to

Silecroft and you will also not be able to use the train to reach here on a Sunday. The station is a request stop. The coastal scrubland around the coast at Silecroft make this a very popular area for the natterjack toad and you could also be treated to the usual wildlife sights of the Cumbria coast such as oyster catchers and terns.

WALK 7
Ravenglass

The only coastal village to be included in the Lake District National Park, Ravenglass is located on the Cumbria Coastal Walk, the long distance path that is the feature of this circular stroll.

Coast path and tide times
This is a loop of the Cumbria Coastal Walk, taking the path that sticks to the tidal River Esk on the way out and heading back to Ravenglass on an alternative route for when the tide is high. It's a lovely route because it allows you to take in part of the coast, nature reserves, farming land and views of fells. But it's important that you check the Whitehaven tide times before heading out. If there is a high tide of more than 7.2 metres, it's possible that part of the outward path will be blocked off for two hours before and two hours after the high tide time.

Ravenglass Roman Bath House
In this remote part of Cumbria, it's quite remarkable to come across a brilliant Roman ruin from the days when soldiers of that long-gone empire were patrolling this area. The whole building would have been around 12 metres wide and 27 metres long when in its full glory, the surviving section being the western end of the bath house. Excavations here started in 1881 and archaeologists now reckon there was a suite of rooms inside, with changing rooms that were designed with little niches to contain statues.

Up Ravenglass! The Roman bath house is passed on the route of the walk

The Romans set up their settlement at Ravenglass in AD 130 and stayed here until the end of the 4th century. The fort itself was built of timber and turf, although a stone wall was later added. The bath house contains external buttresses, possibly to take the weight of the roof. Back then, Ravenglass was known as *Glannoventa*.

Starting point	Ravenglass Train Station, in the centre of Ravenglass at grid reference SD 084,964
Getting there	Sited at the western edge of the Lake District on the Cumbrian coast, Ravenglass can be a slog to reach from the M6. From the south, leave at Junction 36 and follow the A595, while you should leave at Junction 40 if coming from the north, heading beyond Keswick and picking up the A595 south. Once you get to Ravenglass, the road off and train station are well signed. I prefer to go by train and you'll find Ravenglass Station well served by a regular service on the Cumbria Coast Line
Length	5.1km / 3.1 miles
Terrain	1½ hours
Refreshments	A nice walk from the Ravenglass train stations deserves a rest and a drink at the Ratty Arms, the pub adjoining the platform which is named after the Eskdale line. Tel: 01229 717676 www.rattyarms.co.uk CA18 1SN
Difficulty	There is a fairly steep hill to climb halfway along, the rest being on the level. Paths around the coast can be wet and uneven
Map	OS Explorer OL6 The English Lakes South Western Area
Nearest tourist information	Broughton-in-Furness. Tel: 01229 716115
Next stations	The next stop heading south is Bootle and if you're northbound you will come to Drigg shortly after Ravenglass

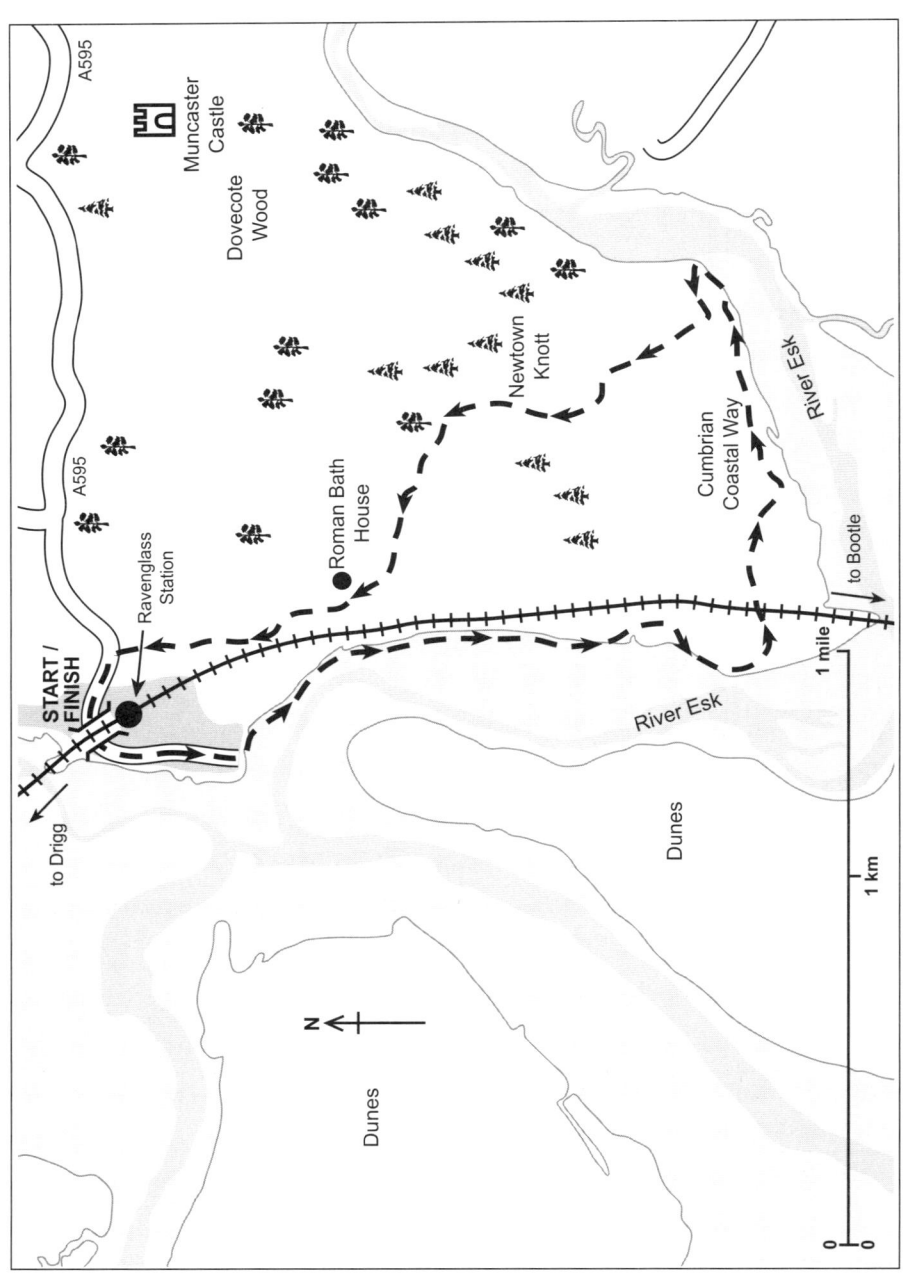

Route

Even if you're at the main Ravenglass Station for the Cumbria Coastline, you may feel like you have gone back in time when you get off the train and can hear the whistling steam trains of the adjoining heritage railway. That charming line, known as La'al Ratty to locals is charming and explored in its own section of this book. But for this walk you need to start off from the northbound platform of the main line, where the Ratty Arms pub is found.

Go into the car park (Grid reference SD 085, 964) and head down to the road, turning left at the junction. Almost immediately you get an insight into the picturesque location of Ravenglass, sandwiched between the fells and the banks of the River Esk. A series of benches on the right allow you to pause and enjoy the boats, dunes and water flowing out to the Irish Sea. The vast offshore wind farm visible out to sea presents a 21st century feel to the view, though I feel it adds more that it detracts.

Heading into Ravenglass, turn right onto Croftlands Drive which keeps you running alongside the river. You'll pass a series of places

You venture on part of the Cumbrian Coastal Way

to grab a drink here by this lovely stretch of buildings. When you get to the end of the road, turn left and keep to the path at the top of the river bank as it goes past houses on the left. This brings you out at a track, but look out for a path on the right after a wall that takes you up a grassy bank (SD 085, 961). You now follow the path for some time as it skirts the edge of the River Esk. As you can see from the amount of driftwood on the path and the odd maritime artefact such as a lobster net, the water can reach the path on very high tides so heed the warning at the start of this chapter which suggests you check tide times.

On this section of the walk, you get a clear view on the right of Eskmeals Dunes Nature Reserve and if you keep an eye out you may see a good deal of bird life, including oyster catchers on the shore. After some time, the route of the river bends round to the left and you follow the path that takes you under the railway track at grid reference SD 088, 948. You can get a good view here of Eskmeals Viaduct, one of several that had to be built to allow trains easier access to the peninsulas of the southern and western Lake District. Along this part of the walk, you're also able to enjoy views of the sea as well as the western fells in an area of the National Park that in my opinion is under-rated and doesn't get anything like the visitor numbers of the central fells.

With the woodland of the small Beacon Plantation on your left, continue along the Cumbria Coastal Path with the River Esk on your right. Take care on this section of the walk, which can be wet after heavy rain or following a high tide. You need to keep looking out for a large gate on your left when you reach a wooden pole in the middle of the path (grid reference SD 097, 949). Go through the gate, turning left onto the track and picking up the other part of this Cumbria Coastal Path loop. After a short time, take the sharp turn on the right and climb the small hill towards Newtown Knott, keeping to the left of the peak. Head into the next field, keeping the large stone wall on your right and begin heading down the hill. Have a look out to sea here, for on a clear day you'll be able to see out to the Isle of Man.

At the bottom of the field go through a gate and the past buildings of Newtown, turning on the track signed for Ravenglass. As you reach the a road, turn right onto it and you'll soon find yourself walking past the Roman Bath House, a remarkable ruin from the days when the Roman Empire stretched up to Hadrian's Wall. Continuing along the road, you'll pass a camp site on the right before coming out at a road. Here, take the path on the left which takes you down to the railway line. On the far side of the bridge, go through the kissing gate which takes you down to the Ratty Arms, where the walk started.

Snow is on the fells, but spring is in the air!

WALK 8
St Bees

Few train stations are so close to dramatic coastal scenery, making this cliff-top walk a wonderful place to escape the hustle and bustle of Lakeland towns via public transport.

Coast to Coast Walk
It was the famous Lake District fell-walker and author Alfred Wainwright who devised the Coast to Coast Walk, outlining his preferred route in a 1973 book. In it, he suggests that those attempting it place a foot into the Irish Sea at St Bees before they set off and dip a toe in the North Sea when it's completed several days later at Robin Hood's Bay. Due to several reasons, including busy roads and erosion, the actual route chosen by Wainwright has been altered a little and the book has been revised a few times to keep it updated. But the principal remains the same – to experience a cross-section of England from west to east, cutting through some fantastic landscapes of the Lake District, Yorkshire Dales and North York Moors. At 182 miles in length, the walk is demanding and needs considerable planning before you take your first steps. Wainwright describes it in 12 sections, so following this will allow it to be done during a two week holiday. Although it's an unofficial route and remains unsigned along much of the passage, most of it is along well-established routes, including The Cleveland Way. It's a two week trek that sees you leaving the sea behind you and walking towards the sea, which is quite an exciting challenge.

St Bees
Apart from being the chosen location to step out onto the Coast to Coast path, St Bees is significant for a number of other reasons, not least being one of the important train station stops on the west coast of Cumbria. On this walk from St Bees you will also pass along the only real cliff top between Scotland and Wales, making it a prominent landform amongst miles of coast that gentle slips away to the sea.

It also boasts the only section of Heritage Coastline in Cumbria, is a Site of Special Scientific Interest and a home to the largest seabird colony in the north-west, making it a hotspot for birdwatchers flocking to the RSPB site.

Perhaps the biggest change to the village came in 1849 when the railway station opened, enabling people who lived in nearby towns and villages to use St Bees as a commuter settlement. But it also saw the growth of the local quarrying business and the railway was an ideal method to transport huge quantities of local sandstone to Barrow to be used in construction. Although trade has fallen from its peak, there are still quarries operating in the area today. The Victorian Railway also brought tourists and made it popular for those wanting a coastal escape; within two years of the Furness Railway line opening, local hotels had even attracted the Lord Mayor of London for a short break. Tourists still use the stop today, many of them coming to walk over the impressive St Bees Head or, rather more ambitiously, begin their lengthy journey to Robin Hood's Bay.

One unique feature of the St Bees coastline at low spring tides is the wreck of Spanish steamship *SS Izaro*, which ran aground in thick fog carrying iron ore to Maryport in May 1907. The crew, from Bilbao, lived on the nearby rocks for a while until it emerged the ship could not be re-floated. One hundred years to the day after the incident, the anchor was salvaged from the wreck and placed along with an information board on the seafront at St Bees.

Historical view of how the station used to be *(photograph: Ben Brooksbank)*

Starting point	The train station at St Bees is easy to find in the village on the B5345, at grid reference NX 970, 119
Getting there	Lying in the north-west of the Lake District, St Bees can take a long time to reach when you're leaving the M6. The best bet is to leave the motorway at Junction 40 and drive beyond Keswick, following signs for Cockermouth and then Whitehaven on the A595. Once south of Whitehaven, you'll see a sign for St Bees on the right. St Bees train station is found in the centre of the village, at grid reference (NX 970, 119). This is a great walk to do when you arrive on the train, but if you are coming by car there is a car park at the train station. However, you may find it easier to head for the car park at St Bees' beach, missing out the first section of the walk from the station to the sea
Length	10.2km / 6.3miles
Terrain	3 hours
Refreshments	The Queens Hotel is a 17th century pub in the centre of the village with real ale, good meals and accommodation. Tel: 01946 822287 CA26 0DE www.marstonpubs.co.uk/queenshotelcumbria
Difficulty	There are some steep climbs along the cliff top path
Map	OS Explorer OL4 The English Lakes: North-Western Area
Nearest tourist information	Market Place, Whitehaven Tel: 01946 598914
Next stations	Heading north from St Bees brings you to the wonderfully named Corkickle, while Nethertown lies to the south

Route

From the train station at St Bees, head from the platform to the main road and turn left onto it. Take a sharp left at the side of the station and follow this road for the best part of a kilometre until it brings you

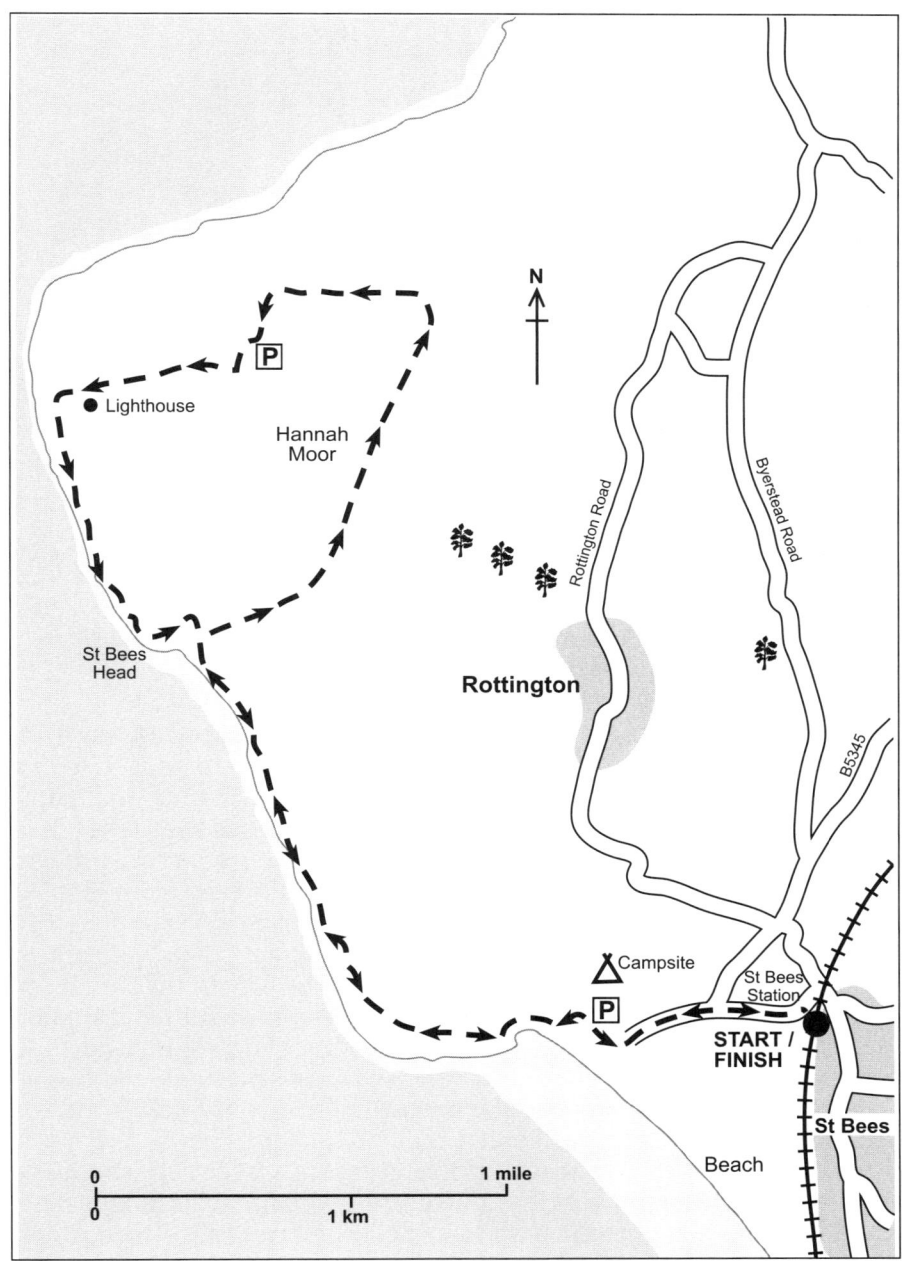

out at the sea. Whilst not a bustling seaside resort in the traditional sense, there are things to explore here and these include a café and the information about the *SS Izaro* shipwreck.

You eventually need to be heading to the promenade and turning right along it, following the sign for 'Cliff Walkers' and heading for the wooden footbridge which takes you over Rottington Beck, then straight on up the hill. There are a series of gates to head through along this section, but the walk is fairly straightforward and the trickiest part is the steep ascent. Keep back from the edge of the cliff to avoid unwanted accidents, although the prickly gorse does a fairly sound job at keeping walkers away from it in places.

St Bees is still a functioning, popular train station, with many using it as a method of starting the Coast to Coast walk

At the brow of the hill the lighthouse comes into view and there are some very impressive sights along the cliff and out to sea. There's a bench on the corner at the top along with some information and maps, explaining that the view west on a clear day includes the Isle of Man and Scotland can often by seen to the north. To the south, you can see the lines of groynes protecting the beach at St Bees from erosion and, further in the distance, the Sellafield complex.

This is the route of the Coast to Coast Walk as it heads out of St Bees and winds an uncompromising path all the way to the North Sea at Robin Hood's Bay. Once you're on the cliff top it's a pretty easy walk along the tops, calling on you to head through the occasional gate and generally just stick to the path, which is unsurprisingly well used given that it's on such a popular long distance route and is such a prominent headland in these parts.

Before long, when you reach grid reference NX 945, 134, you'll see a path off to the right, which you need to take and head inland. This climbs up the hill, over Hannah Moor, bending round to the left and

Looking down to the sands of St Bees, with the groynes on the beach that aim to stop beach erosion

eventually bringing you out at a track which you need to head straight ahead on. This track takes you by a mast on the right and soon after that you'll see a track on the left, which you should take. At this point, you are 126 metres above sea level, which is a fairly impressive climb you've done given that you were at sea level not long ago.

Follow this road as it turns sharply left and goes past Tarnflat Hall and a campsite on the way to the lighthouse. Beyond this working lighthouse, at the northern side of St Bees Head, you will come to the coast path, and here turn left onto it, heading south. The slow descent continues until you cross the stream and begin to rise at the other side.

It's worth pointing out that all the while you will be able to see some of the fabulous bird life that makes a home on these cliffs. Head along the well-used track on the cliff-top, retracing your footsteps on this section of the walk as you proceed around the southern end of the headland back down to St Bees.

Descending the final sections of the cliff, it's quite striking to see how much of St Bees is actually taken up by holiday caravans and this explains why this relatively remote coastal village is often fairly busy in the summer months.

Once you're down at the bottom, cross over the footbridge and make your way through the car park to the main road and follow it away from the sea. You'll soon come to a fork in the road and you should turn right on the road that will take you back to the train station where you set out from.

WALK 9
Ravenglass to Irton Road

A delightful one-way walk that sets out from Ravenglass, heads over the fells and winds up at Irton Road, leaving you with a lovely steam rail journey back to the coast. Check the times of the trains from Irton Road before you set out!

The heritage railway at Ravenglass is the perfect place to step back in time and experience the charm of working steam engines

Starting point	Ravenglass Train Station, at grid reference SD 084, 964
Getting there	The starting point for this walk is Ravenglass and the train is a good way to reach it, positioned as it is halfway along the Cumbria Coast Line. Driving to Ravenglass from the motorway always seems to take longer than you originally think. Head for the coastal

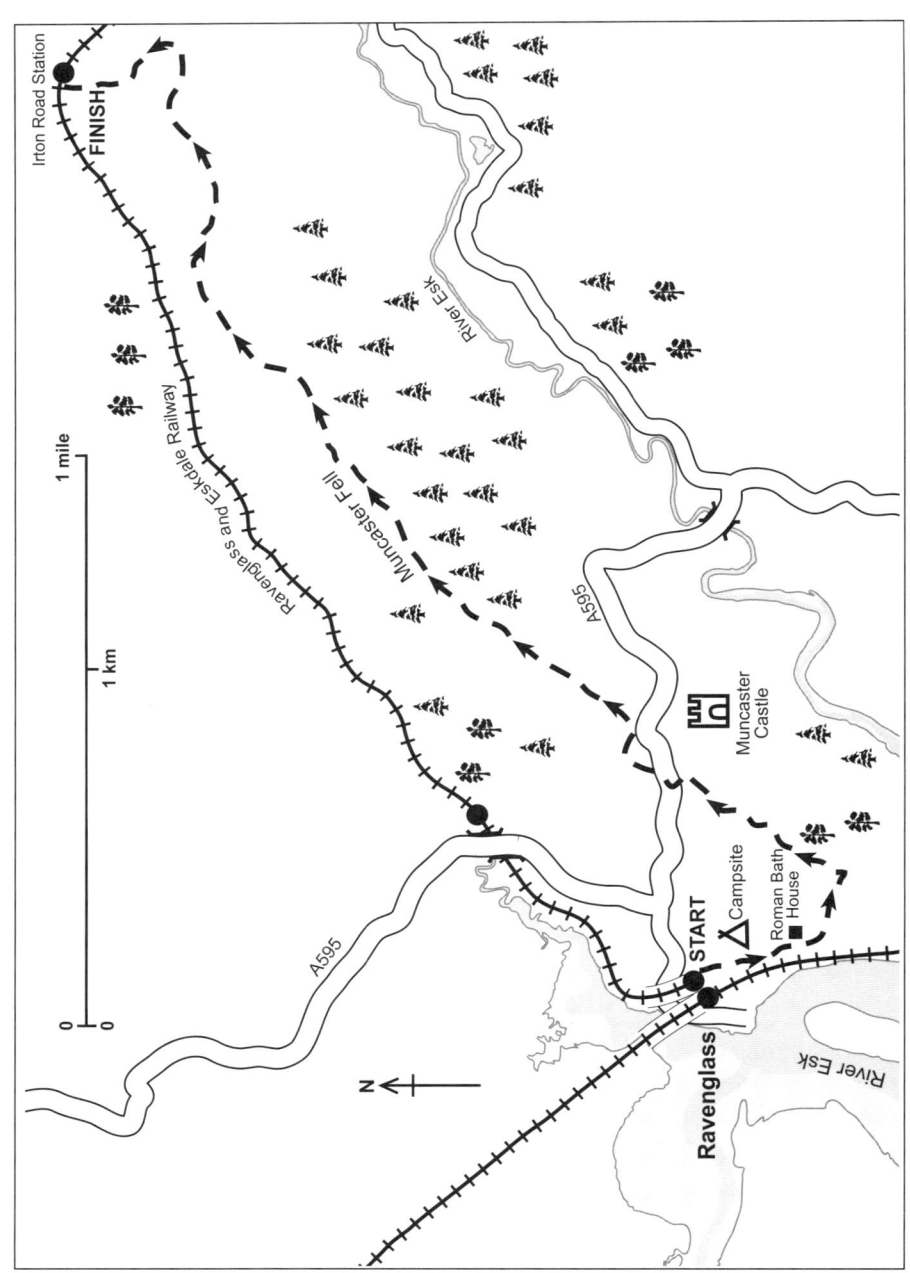

Getting there (cont'd)	road that skirts the western side of the Lake District, leaving from Junction 40 of the M6 if you're coming from the north and Junction 36 if you're coming from the south
Length	5 miles
Terrain	3½ hours
Refreshments	At Eskdale Green you'll find a fine pub called King George IV Inn, which offers food and drink as well as a range of accommodation. Tel: 01946 723470 CA19 1TS www.kinggeorge-eskdale.co.uk
Difficulty	Some moderate climbs on good paths
Map	OS Explorer OL4 The English Lakes South Western Area
Nearest tourist information	The Old Town Hall, Broughton-in-Furness. Tel: 01229 716115
Next stations	A short distance from Irton Road, the next stop east is The Green, while you'll come to Murthwaite Halt on the way down to Ravenglass in the west. Ravenglass is located between Drigg and Bootle stations on the main line

Route

Whether you're starting out from the main Ravenglass Station or the smaller heritage line of the Ravenglass and Eskdale Railway, make your way to the footbridge that goes over the lines. From the main Cumbria coastal line, continue straight ahead across here and enter the footpath. From the narrow gauge railway, turn left onto the footpath when you reach the bridge. Continue ahead until you come to a road, but at this point turn right onto a track that will take you by a camping and caravan site on the left. Head beyond this and through some woods, still sticking to the well marked track, and soon you will find yourself passing the rather wonderful and very understated Roman Bath House ruins.

Just beyond this, turn left at a fork in the path (SD 089, 957). You're now beginning a gradual uphill climb. Just after passing under the power lines, take the path on the left and follow it through the wood and by a stream, heading by a pond on your way up. This will eventually bring you out into the grounds of Muncaster Castle, where you should keep your eyes out for an archway leading you out onto the main A595 road. Cross over here and take the path directly across the road, to the right of the car park.

After a short walk you take a track off to the right, which is at a right angle to the one you are on. This once again brings you out onto the A595, but just before you reach the road you will take the path on the left, known as Fell Lane, which starts to climb a little steeper. This is a very straight route at first and you should ignore turnings off to the left and right and proceed straight ahead, passing Tarn Wood on your right and Muncaster Tarn on your left. Continue straight ahead and pass through a gate; you then have a wood on your left and when this comes to an end you find yourself out on Muncaster Fell.

Hooker Crag rises up to the left, the triangulation pillar on the top signalling that point to be 231 metres above sea level, but stick to the path that goes straight ahead, with the enclosed woods away to your right. The path bends round to the left and climbs up, here being where the views really come into their own and a glorious panorama opens out.

The descent from Muncaster Fell begins now, a fairly simple and straightforward one that follows this path, passing the heights of Silver Knott on the left and then passing close to Rabbit How. The path eventually brings you out at a junction, where you should turn left onto the track that passes in front of you at grid reference SD 139, 993. This path continues beyond a couple of farms and after around 750 metres it will bring you out at Irton Road Station, where you can get a train back to Ravenglass.

Irton Road and Eskdale Green Railway Stations

Although it's just ten miles to the west of Coniston, Eskdale Green has a feel of being very much on the fringes of the Lake District, near to the coast and the railway 'goings on' at Ravenglass. In fact, the Ravenglass and Eskdale Railway actually has two stations situated in the village, and several of the stations on the line have had to change their name in the past to overcome growing confusion. Eskdale Green, five miles from Ravenglass and two miles from the terminus at Dalegarth, used to be known as King Of Prussia because it was close to a pub going by the same name, but then changed to Eskdale Green.

Thousands have enjoyed a sunny day out on the open-top carriages of La'al Ratty

However, at that time, the terminus was called Eskdale (Dalegarth) and led to misunderstanding so the name of the Eskdale Green station changed simply to The Green in the 1960s. It switched back to Eskdale Green in 2007 when the new terminus opened and was named Dalegarth for Boot.

The other station to be found in Eskdale Green was originally called Hollowstones, named after a farm close by. But this was changed to Irton Road, which is appropriate as it's on the road that goes to Irton. At this station there are sidings and an engine shed, which often houses vehicles not being used by the heritage railway. It was once home to engines working at the nearby quarry, though today you are more likely to see the sleigh used for Santa Specials. But only when the jolly old elf is not in need of it.

WALK 10
Beckfoot

The walks from the stations in this part of the Lake District give a perfect opportunity to sample one of the most scenic heritage railway lines in the country.

Ravenglass and Eskdale Railway Preservation Society

Once you've travelled from Ravenglass to Dalegarth, many become smitten with this picturesque valley and are determined to make a return visit as soon as possible. And, if you find yourself falling in love with the Ravenglass and Eskdale Railway while trekking from Beckfoot or Dalegarth on this walk, you may be interested in heading back to the stations as a volunteer.

Whether it's installing a fence, litter picking or assisting with engineering, the railway relies on a host of volunteers to keep the trains running smoothly. Perhaps the most appealing role is that of a platform guard, giving you the chance to make sure all the passengers are on board, check that the signal is off and blow your whistle to get the train moving. Full training is given for all the jobs you'll have to undertake on the journey as well as using the walkie talkies. Virtually all the guarding roles are filled with volunteers who have been trained to couple and uncouple trains and carry out vital customer service duties, such as telling interested passengers the history of the line. For more information about volunteering on the railway, check out the website **www.rerps.co.uk**

Steam Locomotives

The railway that takes you on the seven mile journey from Ravenglass has four steam engines, so you stand a decent chance of chugging along on one of these. This is a route that can almost transport you back in time to the days of steam as well as getting you to Dalegarth. Three of the four steam locomotives are named after rivers, the oldest of which is the *River Irt* which was built in 1894 by Sir Arthur Heywood. In 1923 the *River Esk* was built specifically for the railway to shift granite from the quarry at Beckfoot and it still operates along the line. Then, in 1966, the Preservation Society built *River Mite* and

It's a journey back in time as well as voyage to Ravenglass
(photograph: Ben Brooksbank)

for the centenary celebrations in 1976 *Northern Rock* was built in the railway's own Ravenglass workshops. The design for this engine was so successful that it was used again to build a couple of engines for a Japanese railway, these now running as *Northern Rock II* and *Cumbria*. There are also five diesel locomotives working the route, so take a look out for *Douglas Ferreira, Lady Wakefield, Perkins, Shelagh of Eskdale* and *Cyril*.

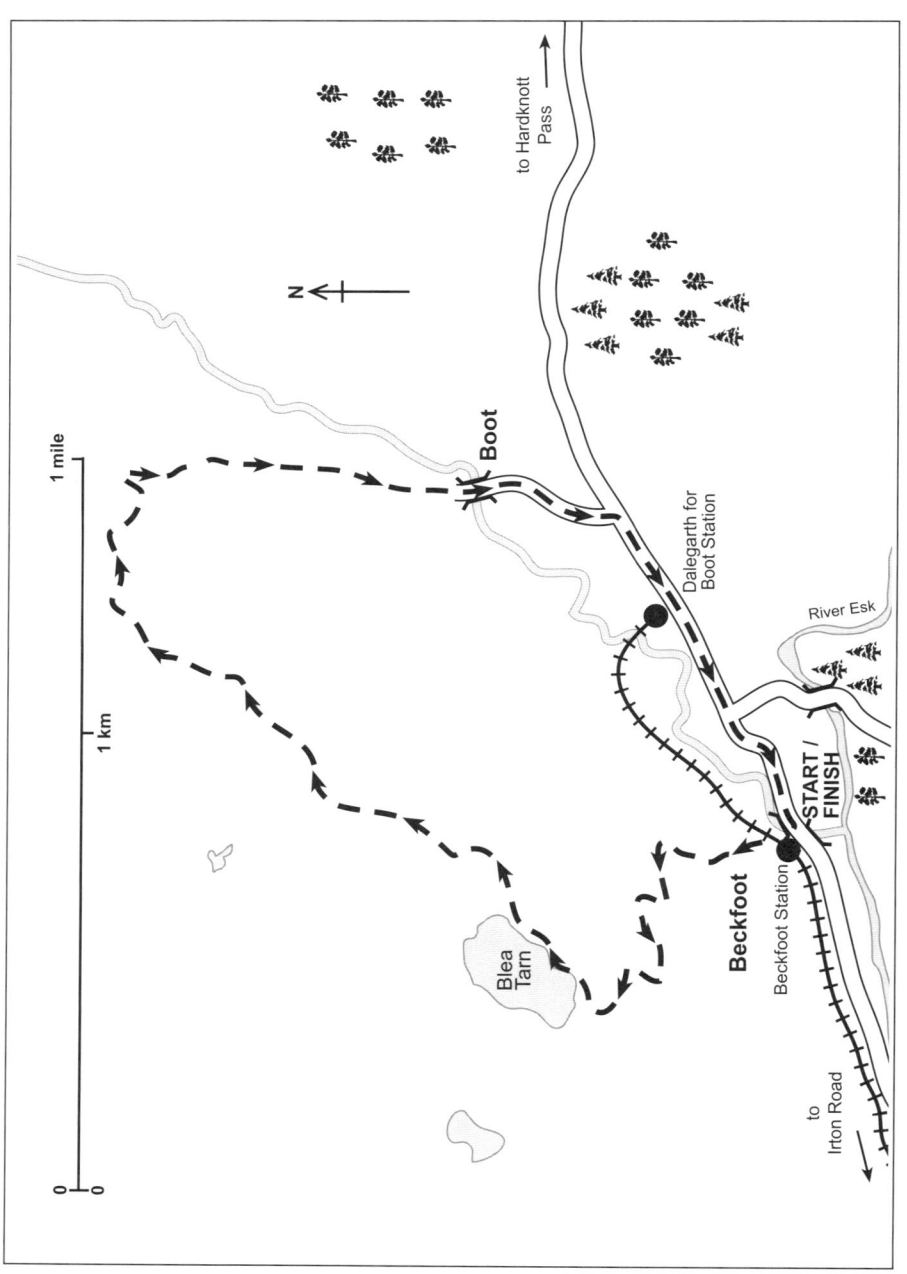

Starting point	Beckfoot Train Station at grid reference NY 168, 004
Getting there	From the heart of the Lakes, head to Ambleside and follow the A593 to Coniston, turning off for Little Langdale and the Wrynose and Hardknott passes just after Clappersgate. At the other end of the passes, you'll reach Beckfoot. Approaching from the north or south, it may be easier to head for the coastal A595, where the turning for Dalegarth (and so Beckfoot) is just north of Ravenglass. Of course, you can also take the steam train from Ravenglass to Beckfoot
Length	4.4km / 2.8 miles
Terrain	1¾ hours
Refreshments	From Beckfoot, it's a short walk into Boot where you can enjoy the food and drink available at Brook House Inn. Tel: 019467 23288 CA19 1TG www.brookhouseinn.co.uk
Difficulty	A steep climb from the outset, then a steady descent over the fells
Map	OS Explorer OL6 The English Lakes South Western Area
Nearest tourist information	Coniston. Tel: 015394 41533
Next stations	Heading north-west you'll reach the steam railway terminus at Dalegarth for Boot, while if you head from here to Ravenglass the next request stop will be Fisherground

Route

When you are at Beckfoot Station (grid reference NY 168, 004) you need to cross over the track away from the station and pick up the path that heads up the hill, going through the gate. The path is signed to Blea Tarn and you start climbing up the path, keeping the stone wall on the right. This is an easy path to follow and it twists and turns over rocky ground. As so often in the Lake District, climbing the path gives the most incredible views. This route is no exception and as you climb you'll be able to keep an eye on Beckfoot Station at the bottom of the hill, and follow the track a few hundred metres up the valley as it bends into Dalegarth Station. As the path continues to meander up the hill you eventually reach a brow which affords a fabulous panorama out to the Irish Sea.

You'll soon reach a junction of paths by a small cairn, where you should take the path to the right and follow it as it bends round to the left. As the path levels out a little, you pass a ruined building on the left. The path will bring you out at Blea Tarn, which is wonderfully hidden up the fell until you are very close to it. When you reach it, turn right onto the path which heads around the tarn.

With the water still on your left, follow the path around the perimeter of the tarn and then stick to it as it leaves the water and climbs into the hills once again, giving you a wonderful view down onto Blea Tarn. Continue on the path and head by cairn markers as you begin a steady descent down the hill and over a small stream via a few stepping stones. Continue straight ahead and you will eventually come to a junction of paths, marked by a small cairn on the right, at a point when you can see Eel Tarn across to the right on the other side of the valley.

Take this path (NY 176, 018) that heads down to the right and you will soon find yourself walking among a series of ruined buildings which are a reminder of a time when this part of the Lake District was worked to get iron ore out of mines. Indeed, the working area you are now walking through is the reason that the railway at the bottom of the hill was actually built in the first place. The path that you are on eventually turns into a track

Ruined buildings are a reminder of the area's industrial past

Blea Tarn is the reward for those climbing the hill from the station

and you head over a small stream. As you continue down the hill, you'll come to a gate. Press on ahead and you will find yourself in the village of Boot. Follow the road straight ahead, passing an old mill building on the left and the Boot Inn on the right. When you reach the T-junction, turn right and head along the road. Pass Dalegarth Station on the right and continue ahead for approximately 350 metres until you reach Beckfoot Station, where the walk started.

WALK 11
Dalegarth for Boot

An incredible setting awaits you even before you've set off on the walk, this circular route takes you to one of the Lake District's most spectacular waterfalls.

Dalegarth for Boot Station

The terminus at the eastern end of the Ravenglass and Eskdale Railway used to be a little further towards Boot, close to the cottages that used to house local miners. But when the line was converted from 3 foot gauge to 15 foot gauge, the smaller engines had trouble with the gradient on the way to Boot. So, in the mid-1920s, it was decided to relocate the station a small way along what used to be a mining branch line to the cottages at Gill Force.

The Dalegarth For Boot station was a converted hut from a weapons testing site at Ravenglass for about 80 years, but in 2007 the modern

Dalegarth Station in 1951 *(photograph: Ben Brooksbank)*

station building was constructed and it is now home to a café, shopping area and education room.

When it was officially opened, the prestigious ceremonial job fell to music producer and railway enthusiast Pete Waterman, famous for

Starting point	The station this walks leaves from is at the terminus of the heritage railway in Haverthwaite, grid reference SD 349, 842
Getting there	From the heart of the Lakes, head to Ambleside and follow the A593 to Coniston, turning off for Little Langdale and the Wrynose and Hardknott passes just after Clappersgate. At the other end of the passes, you'll reach Dalegarth. Approaching from the north or south, it may be easier to head for the coastal A595, where the turning for Dalegarth is just north of Ravenglass. Or make your way to Ravenglass and get the heritage railway up to the terminus
Length	3.7km / 2.3 miles
Terrain	1½ hours
Refreshments	Walking into Boot from Dalegarth, you'll come to the The Boot Inn, offering food, drink and accommodation. www.bootinneskdale.co.uk Tel: 01946 723711 Postcode: CA19 1TG. A short drive towards the Hardknott Pass is the welcoming bar of the Woolpack Inn. www.woolpack.co.uk Tel: 01946 723230 Postcode: CA19 1TH
Difficulty	Some steep sections with bumpy ground. Take care near the waterfall and observe warning signs
Map	OS Explorer OL6 The English Lakes South Western Area
Nearest tourist information	Coniston. Tel: 015394 41533
Next stations	Dalegarth for Boot is the final station on the line, but heading out towards Ravenglass the next station is just a few hundred metres away at Beckfoot, the starting point for another walk in this book

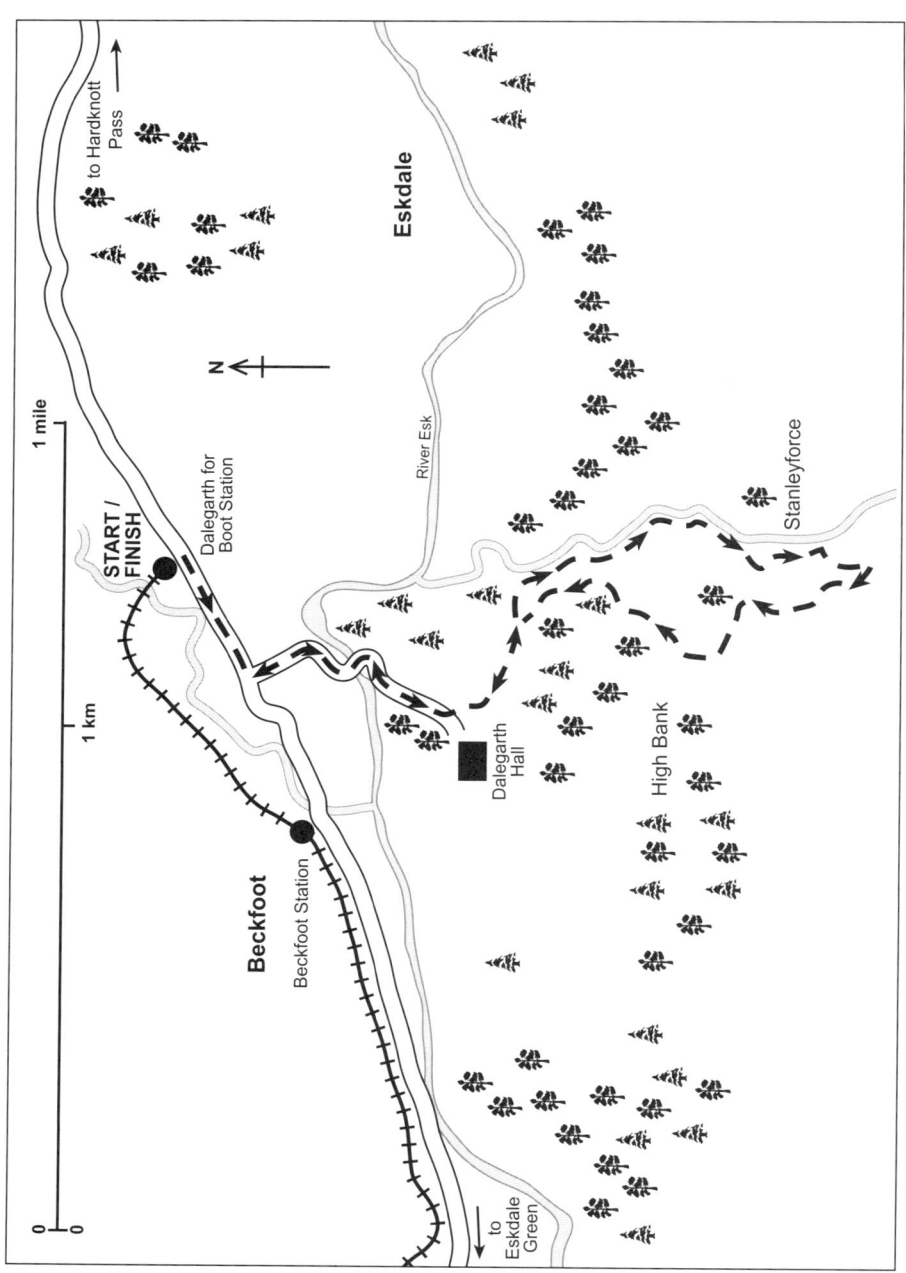

the string of hit singles he had as part of Stock Aitkin and Waterman.

If you should be so lucky as to take a trip on the railway in fine weather, you may get a glimpse of Scafell, the highest mountain in England. It's a great day out, whether you're more interested in the scenery and a drink in the café or you want to get your boots dirty on one of the many fantastic walks around the fells.

Ravenglass and Eskdale Railway

The origins of this wonderfully scenic and atmospheric line date back to 1875 when a transport route was needed to get iron ore from the area around Boot to the coast at Ravenglass.

A year later the trains were carrying passengers into this corner of the Lake District and things were looking rosy. But the happy times were not to last; the line was not making enough money and went bankrupt in 1897. Services continued despite this, but the Ravenglass to Eskdale Railway was closed in 1913. The line was unused for two years but in 1915 it was bought by two narrow gauge enthusiasts who used it for testing locomotives.

When the line next changed hands it was to aid the quarrying in the area, rocks being taken from nearby Beckfoot to Murthwaite, where it was crushed and used for road stone. The Keswick Granite Company later ran raw materials along the tracks, but stopped operations in 1953 and it became difficult to find a buyer for the line when it came up for sale in the late 1950s. Although passenger services had continued to run every year apart from during the war, it was announced that 1960 would be the final operating year and the Ravenglass and Eskdale Railway went under the hammer.

At the auction, Midlands stockbroker Colin Gilbert and local landowner Sir Wavell Wakefield joined forces with the Ravenglass and Eskdale Railway Preservation Society to secure the purchase. Since then, new locomotives have been added to the collection and a visitor centre built at Dalegarth, ensuring that the tourists continue to flock to this great little railway at both ends of the line.

Route

From Dalegarth For Boot Station (grid reference NY 173, 007), head to the road and turn right onto it, following the sign for Dalegarth Falls. Walk along the road, taking care to watch out for traffic on what can be a fairly busy, if remote, rural route. Before long you'll pass a transport company on the right, a seemingly unusual place to store

This is a walk with some great natural features to pass along the way

holiday coaches. Soon after this, look out for a path off to the left signed to Stanley Ghyll Force half a mile away. Go over a bridge, taking time to look over to a really deep part of the river, before pressing on along the road, passing a car park a little further up on the left.

Heading into woodland, you'll soon see a track off to the right which you should ignore, instead following the sign for Waterfalls that sends you off to the left. Go through a gate before continuing straight ahead on the path, following signs for the Waterfalls, Stanley Ghyll and Birker Fell. With pine trees rising into the sky, the babbling of the river greeting your ears and wonderful fell landscape surrounding you, this walk gets better and better as you approach the falls. Before long you'll see a sign pointing you off to the left in search of 'Waterfalls' and this will take you into the Stanley Ghyl access area (NY 172, 000).

You're now heading up the valley on the right hand side of the river, making your way through beautiful woodland with a range of trees. Continue walking up by the side of the river until you reach a wooden footbridge, which you should make your way across and then head up the valley on the left of the river. Shortly after there are two more wooden footbridges, meaning you walk for a while on the right of the river again before once more crossing to the left. This will take you up to the waterfall, though you must take care of the drops and rocks when you visit and be responsible.

When you've finished gazing at this marvellous natural feature, and one of the finest waterfalls in the Lakes, retrace your footsteps and journey down over the first footbridge. But before you reach the second one, watch out for a steep path off to the left, which enters a rocky set of steps. Climb the steps, keeping a smaller stream on your left this time.

When you reach the top of the hill, cross over the stream and begin a climb to a spectacular viewing point of the waterfalls and fells off in the distance. Take note, however, that there is a 150 foot drop at this point and there is nothing like the fencing and security measures that are now common place on other waterfalls walks.

From just outside the viewing area, turn right and head over a stile into a field, heading straight out towards a wooden marker that signals your discovery of a farming track that you need to turn right onto (grid reference NY 173, 993). Go through a gate, enjoying on this stretch the fabulous views of Eskdale stretching out in front of you. Head through a gate at the bottom and you'll find yourself on a large, wide farming track. At the bottom of this, you'll see the path that you went straight on at earlier on in the walk, and here you should follow the main track as it bends round to the left and retraces your footsteps back to the road. Once at the junction, turn right onto the road and keep going until you reach the station on your left.

Dwindling patches of snow signal the changing of seasons on the Lake District fells

WALK 12
Lakeside

A circular walk through woodland which also gives you the chance to complete the last section by steam train.

Lakeside Station
Opened in 1872 and serving the village of Lakeside, this was once the terminus of the branch line that led from the Furness Railway at Ulverston. Linking a relatively remote part of the Lake District to the main rail network, it helped local settlements to develop as well as providing another route into the region for tourists wanting to spend time near Windermere.

Lakeside is at the southern end of Windermere and when the branch line was completed the tourists of the day were in for another treat because the Furness Railway also bought the Windermere Steam Yacht

Trains packed with tourists still make the steam-powered journey to the station and then head out onto the water thanks to the link with nearby boats

A ticket combining the train and boat provides a genuinely thrilling way to experience the Lake District

Company and so made boat trips link up with the train services. Over the next few decades, no less than nine steam boats operated on Windermere, including the *Rothay* which was built in Lancaster and the *Teal*, constructed in Barrow with capacity for 326 passengers.

Today, the Lakeside and Haverthwaite Railway operates a section of this branch line, which still terminates at Lakeside, and combined tickets can be bought to enjoy a similar Windermere boating experience as 19th century visitors through the private company, Windermere Lake Cruises.

Back when the trains were running along the full length of the branch line, Lakeside Station had two platforms and a roof which covered them both. That fell into disrepair when the line was closed in 1965 as part of the Beeching Axe, and eventually British Rail took away the roof and demolished the clock tower that also stood there, as well as selling off the boating company. The late 1960s, then, were an uneasy time for Lakeside Station and most of it was knocked down, leaving little of the original structure for today's visitors to enjoy. It was not until the early 1970s that trains were once again chugging along as part of the heritage railway movement that slowly started to claw back some of Beeching's redundant track.

The railway in popular culture

Several films and TV series have used the heritage railway as a setting, not surprising when you see if for yourself and imagine how you could have been transported back in time. Lakeside is perhaps the most popular station, given its proximity to the lake, and has actually been renamed as Windermere in several programmes. Of course, there is a real Windermere railway station, but it is not close by the water's edge and does not have the quaint appeal of Lakeside.

In the first year of reopening in 1973, *Swallows and Amazons* was shot at Lakeside and subsequently released a year later, while episodes of *Sherlock Holmes* and Agatha Christie's *Poirot* were also given the Lakeside treatment. In 2007, the Furness Railway earned an historic part in classic locomotive fiction when it featured in the 41st book of the Railway Stories. Written by The Rev. W. Auden's son, Christopher, *Thomas and Victoria* was published in 2007 and introduced the character of *Victoria*, a blue Furness Railway four-wheeled coach.

Windermere

The origins of England's largest lake can be traced back 13,000 years to the last major ice age. This long, thin ribbon lake was created by two glaciers, one of which was in the Troutbeck Valley and the other up at the Fairfield Horseshoe. When they melted, the area which is now home to Windermere started to fill up with water, dammed in place by glacial moraine that was deposited by the glacier.

Some people persist in wrongly calling this stretch of water 'Lake Windermere', when it should be called just 'Windermere'. As the word 'mere' is an Old English term referring to a lake or water, there is no need to put the word 'lake' before Windermere. As with most lakes in the Lake District, such as Ullswater, Coniston Water, Derwent Water or Kentmere, there is no requirement to call it a 'lake' at all. This might seem odd, given that the region is known around the world as The Lake District and is full of lakes, but using the word 'lake' in titles is a Cumbrian *faux pas*. The only time when it is acceptable to assign the word 'lake' to a stretch of water in the Lake District is when talking about Lake Bassenthwaite, which is the only lake in the Lake District to actually have the word 'lake' in name. To be fair, few people go around saying 'Lake Consiton Water' or 'Lake Ullswater', but Windermere is one of the few that does get called 'lake' and there is perhaps good reason for this. For a start, some poets writing about Windermere, such as Millom's famous poet Norman Nicholson, use the term 'Lake Windermere' in their work. There is also the issue of the

Starting point	Lakeside Station, which is found at the southern tip of Windermere, at grid reference SD 378, 873
Getting there	From Junction 36 of the M6, follow signs for Kendal and then take the A590 towards Newby Bridge. Once you're at Newby Bridge, turn right over the narrow bridge and follow the signs for the steam railway. It's also possible to park up at Haverthwaite Station and get the steam train north to Lakeside
Length	3.7km / 2.3 miles
Terrain	1¼ hours
Refreshments	The Lakeside Hotel and Spa is not the cheapest place to grab a drink and a bite to eat after your walk, but some fine choices are available, including coffee in the morning and afternoon tea in the conservatory. Tel: 015396 30001 LA12 8AT www.lakesidehotel.co.uk
Difficulty	There are steep climbs through the woods initially, and take care for the rocks and tree roots on the paths. There is also a small section on a country road without a path
Map	OL7 The Lake District: The South Eastern Area
Nearest tourist information	Brockhole Lake District Visitor Centre. Tel: 015394 46601 Postcode: LA23 1LJ www.brockhole.co.uk
Next station	Lakeside is the northern terminus of the Lakeside and Haverthwaite Railway. The next station heading south is Newby Bridge

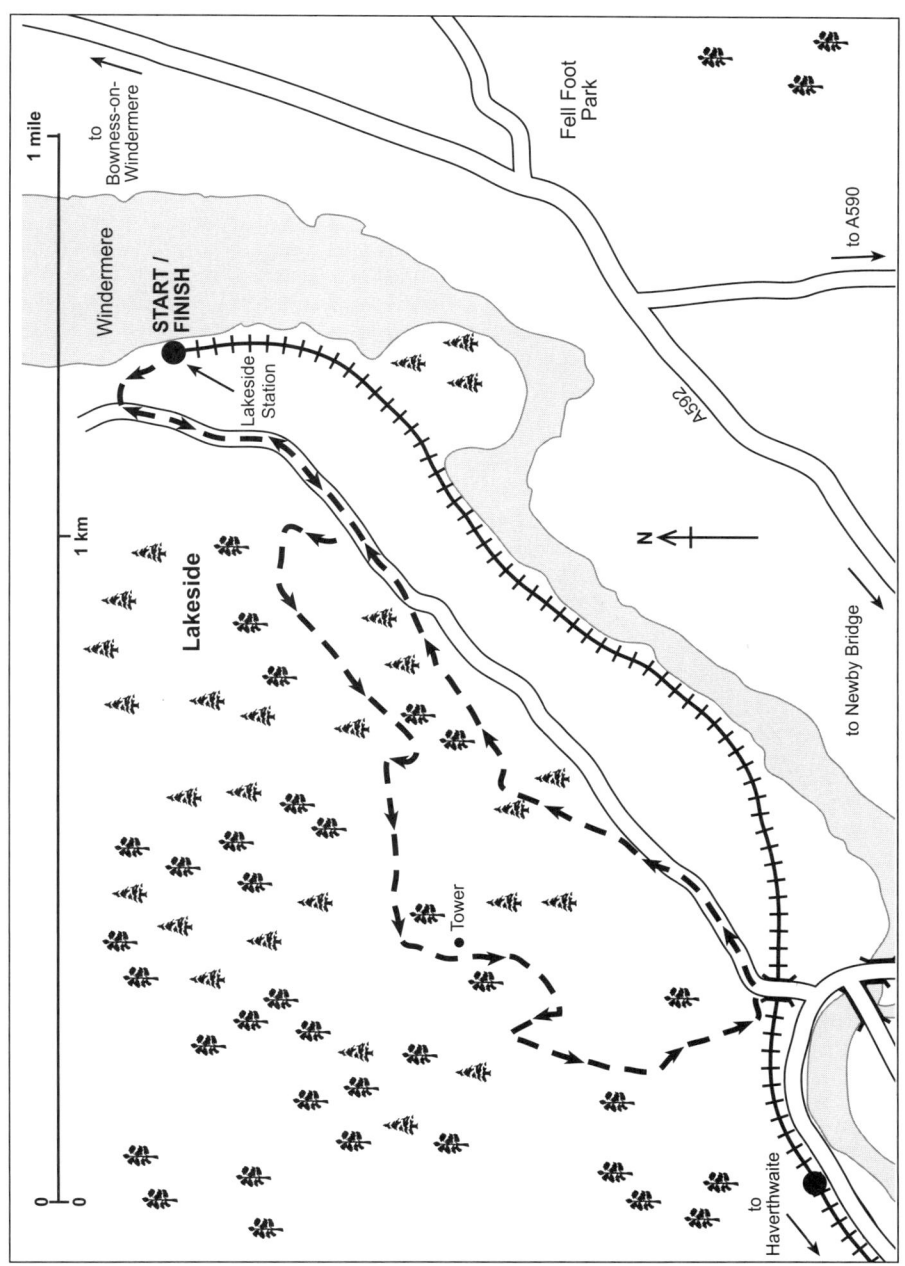

nearby town being called Windermere as well, so using 'Lake Windermere' would help to distinguish whether you mean the urban collection of shops and houses or the expanse of water stretching from Lakeside right up to Ambleside. Confused? If in doubt, try not using the word 'lake' in the Lake District! It's harder than you might think!

Route
From the train station at Lakeside, head for the road which has the Lakeside Hotel on the right and go beyond it to the junction. Turn left here and continue ahead on the road until you leave the village and see a path signed on your right which takes you across a field. Take this and walk slightly to the right across the field, aim for the woods directly across. Climb over the stile here and start on the path through Great Knott Wood (SD 376, 872).

From now on you'll see that there are easy to follow woodland tracks to keep you safely on the route, this one climbing the hill in front of you, steeply at first. Initially you will be following yellow and red signs on wooden posts. The track you are on eventually bends around sharply to the right and stops climbing as sharply. Soon you will come to a junction of paths and you need to follow the white arrow pointing off to the left, up the hill through an old stone wall.

The path continues to climb up the hill, and take a look out here for an amazing array of different mosses on the walls, path and trees. This whole area is part of The Woodland Trust, which plants and manages native trees around the country.

Before long, and quite unexpectedly, the path leads you to a tower, which can be explored by taking a short path branching off to the left. This was built as a monument to Royal Navy officers for the battles fought in the 18th century.

From the tower, head back down to the path that you were on before and turn left onto it, following the yellow arrow sign. Head on through a gap in the wall and then branch right on a path heading down the hill, still located firmly in the woods. As you head down the hill here you move onto some steep, slate steps which can be slippy in wet weather. The path after these steps becomes thinner but keeps heading down, and will then turn to the left.

The path continues to proceed down, passing several holly trees on this section before leaving the woods via a gate (grid reference SD 368, 865). You'll come out onto a path at the bottom, where you should turn left and head towards the road.

The tower in the middle of the woods is incredibly atmospheric

You have a choice here of how to complete the walk, the first being to turn right onto the road and then right again to wind up at Newby Bridge Station. It's possible here, if you time it right, to get the Lakeside and Haverthwaite Railway back up to the starting point at Lakeside. If you do this, you'll need to make sure you check the times on their website **www.lakesiderailway.co.uk**.

Alternatively, if you want to walk back to the station at Lakeside you need to turn left onto the road. After a while, you'll see a path on the left that takes you back into Great Knott Wood, signed for Lakeside. This is a far better option than walking on the road, and it eventually brings you out close to the place where you first entered the wood. Go through the gate onto the road again and turn left, heading back towards the Lakeside Hotel, where a right turn takes you back to the starting point.

WALK 13
Haverthwaite

A walk featuring the Cumbria Coastal Path by the River Leven which returns through woods rich in bluebells during spring.

The Lakeside and Haverthwaite Railway

It was the demand for iron ore that led to the creation of the Furness Railway, with the heavy industries of northern England needing the raw materials that lay on the Cumbrian coast. The railway was built in stages but eventually looped from Carnforth all the way around the coastline and back inland to Carlisle in the north.

With the shipment of iron ore out of Cumbria now enabled, attention turned to helping another booming industry, that of 19th century tourism which was thriving with the introduction of the railways. As early as 1847 the Kendal and Windermere Railway Company opened a branch line to Windermere and by 1866 the decision was taken to add a branch line from Ulverston up to Newby Bridge, with it later being decided to extend the route a mile further north to Lakeside and so allow the link up with the steam boats.

Construction of the railway started in 1867, though delays were commonplace thanks to the difficulty of tunnelling and cutting through the rocks around Haverthwaite. But, on 1st June, 1869, a grand opening ceremony hailed the first operational day of the 7.9 mile route, even though some of the stations along the line were not finished.

The Furness Railway bought the Windermere Steam Yacht Company, allowing passengers to combine the train and boat on their trip, and the branch line was also used for freight such as the coal needed for the steam boats. Everything looked rosy. But by the 1800s, the demand for iron ore was starting to slow. By the time of the First World War, passenger numbers had peaked and the increasing demand for cars after this time meant that the Golden Days were chugging into the distance. In 1938 winter passenger trains were suspended for the first time and would never resume. Though the summer service resumed after World War Two, Haverthwaite and Greenodd Stations were closed in 1946 and, in September 1965, the whole line was shut to passenger traffic.

One of the steam engines at Haverthwaite getting ready for action

The formation and campaigning of the Lakeside Railway Society stopped the line being dismantled and eventually led to the purchase of the section from Haverthwaite to Lakeside in 1970. Initially, it was desired to reopen the whole branch line, but improvements to the A590 were planned and the society could not afford to fund the motorway-style bridges needed to take the road over the track at Haverthwaite. So attention instead turned to the 3.2 miles of track between Haverthwaite and Lakeside, which was eventually restored, repaired and reopened in 1973.

Today, the steam trains running along the short line allow tourists an 18 minute insight into the world of steam. There are a range of tickets available to buy, including ones that combine entry with the Lakeland Motor Museum (**www.lakelandmotormuseum.co.uk**), Windermere Lake Cruises (**www.windermere-lakecruises.co.uk**) and The World of Beatrix Potter (**www.hop-skip-jump.com**) in Windermere.

Haverthwaite Station

Opened in 1869 and serving the nearby passengers living in Haverthwaite, there was also an important freight role at this station. A long siding served the nearby blast furnace at Backbarrow, and the numerous cotton mills that grew up in the area during Victorian times. Backbarrow was also well known for the manufacturing of the ultramarine blue pigment, with a 'blue mill' being nicknamed so locally because dust from it gave much of the village a blue appearance. The station was one of the first to enter a demise and passenger trains stopped calling here in 1946, although they kept passing through en route to Lakeside until 1965. Today it has a new lease of life as a heritage railway that is popular with Lake District tourists.

Be sure to pop into the wonderfully decorated tea rooms at the station

Starting point	The station this walks leaves from is at the terminus of the heritage railway in Haverthwaite, grid reference SD 349, 842
Getting there	From Junction 36 of the M6, head towards Kendal and then take the A590 towards Newby Bridge. Beyond Newby Bridge and Backbarrow, look out for the signs pointing out the station on the right
Length	7.5km / 4.6 miles
Terrain	2¼ hours
Refreshments	Home cooked food and real ales are on offer at the Anglers' Arms in Haverthwaite, which this walks passes twice. Tel: 015395 31216 LA12 8AJ
Difficulty	Much of this walk is on the level, with some modest climbs through the wood
Map	OS Explorer Outdoor Leisure 7. The English Lakes: South Eastern Area
Nearest tourist information	Coronation Hall, County Road, Ulverston. Tel: 01229 587120
Next stations	Haverthwaite is currently the southern terminus for the Lakeside and Haverthwaite Railway, with Newby Bridge being the next stop to the north. In the past, when the railway ventured south towards Ulverston, the next station was Greenodd

Route

From the station at Haverthwaite, leave the site and head for the main road. Turn left on the path until you see the place where you can cross over the busy A590. Take care as you do this as it can be a busy road. Once you're across the road, turn right and walk on the path beside the A590 for a few metres before turning down the road to the left towards Haverthwaite, passing the Anglers' Arms pub on the right.

Continue to walk down this road, noting that the River Leven is to be found down to the left. This is the river that flows out of

87

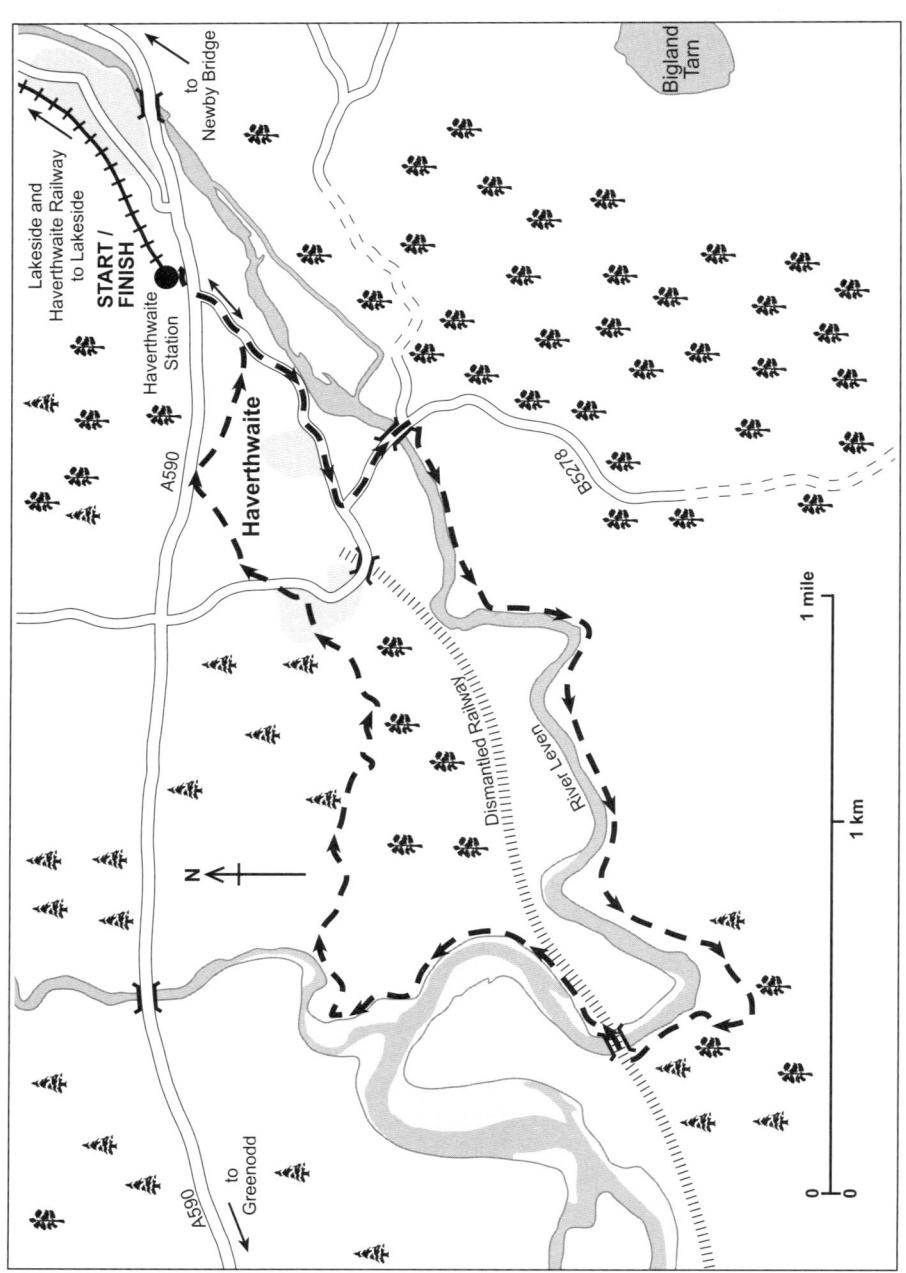

Windermere and much of this walk follows its course. The road bends round to the left, you pick up the B5278 and soon cross over the River Leven. At the far side of the bridge, take the track off to the right which forms a section of the Cumbria Coastal Path. Follow this track until you see a further path on the right which keeps you at the side of the river and on the coastal path. Continue on the path, keeping the river on the right and you'll soon need to cross over a footbridge, which stays hidden until the last moment.

You enter the Holker Estate and a section of the walk right next to the River Leven, which at this point is tidal as it is so close to its point of entry to Morecambe Bay. The scenery at this point is wonderful, enjoying the mountains in the distance and also the flat, glacial landscape at the foot of the fells as the land falls away into the sea. It's a real contrast.

Follow the track, taking the direction of cycle path 70 when you see the sign. You'll eventually enter Roudsea Wood and soon after doing so, at grid reference SD 329, 826, there is a path to the right which you need to take. With the river still sitting down to the right, you'll see a bridge spanning the water up ahead, and you turn right onto the path and go across it. This, as you'll recognise, is part of the old railway route and the bridge used to take engines from the Furness Line up to Lakeside, via Haverthwaite where you set out from. Although the line is now dismantled, access is not allowed to all of it and once you cross the bridge you will see a sign directing you off to the left through a gate.

Cross the field and take the gate on the left when faced with a choice of two at the far side of the field. There is now a definite feel of being close to the coast, backed up by the embankments constructed to withstand high tides, the tidal nature of the river at this point evidenced by the large quantity of driftwood you can see on the path. Sadly, this is combined with the usual sea debris of plastic bottles, tin cans and the odd shoe. I find such litter disturbing in that it's unsightly, but also a little intriguing as it's drifted here with an unknown back story.

The river is now on your left and you should stick to the path, following the top of the embankment as it bends off to the right and drifts a little away from the water. The river on your left now is Rusland Pool and the place where it meets the River Leven is known as Pool Foot. But you need to look out for a path off to the right (grid reference SD 331, 838) which takes you away from the rivers and inland towards Haverthwaite. When you go through a gate into the

The disused track on part of this walk was once the scene of steam trains rattling from Haverthwaite to Ulverston

field, stick to the left and aim for a gate which takes you into a wood. Follow the path through the trees, which in late spring are a good place to spot bluebells.

When you come out of the woods and reach the houses of Haverthwaite, turn right and you'll find yourself at the B5278 once more, where you should turn left. Take the path you'll soon see on the right (SD 341, 84) which takes you across a field and out onto a road. At the end of this little lane, turn left onto the road and you will be brought back to the A590 with Haverthwaite Station across the dual carriageway. The steam railway runs trips up to Newby Bridge and Lakeside, which is the starting point for another walk in this book.

WALK 14
Foxfield to Kirkby-in-Furness

A one-way walk between two railway stations where the Lakeland fells drop down towards Morecambe Bay, this is a great place to stretch your legs and then catch the train back.

Starting point	The starting point is Foxfield Station, at grid reference SD 208, 854
Getting there	By train, Foxfield can be reached via the Furness Line, which runs from Carnforth. To drive, leave the M6 at Junction 36 and follow the signs for Newby Bridge, continuing on the A590 until you can take the A5092 on the right at Greenodd. Foxfield and the train station are signed
Length	5.3km / 3.3 miles
Terrain	1½ hours
Refreshments	You'll find not just a pub but a brewery at The Prince of Wales in Foxfield, home to the Foxfield Brewery. Tel: 01229 716238 LA20 6BX www.princeofwalesfoxfield.co.uk
Difficulty	Largely flat and easy to follow paths
Map	OS Explorer OL7 The English Lakes South Eastern Area
Nearest tourist information	Broughton Information Centre, The Old Town Hall, The Square, Broughton-in-Furness, 01229 716115
Next stations	Heading towards Barrow you'll next come to The Green, while Kirkby-in-Furness lies on the route back to Grange

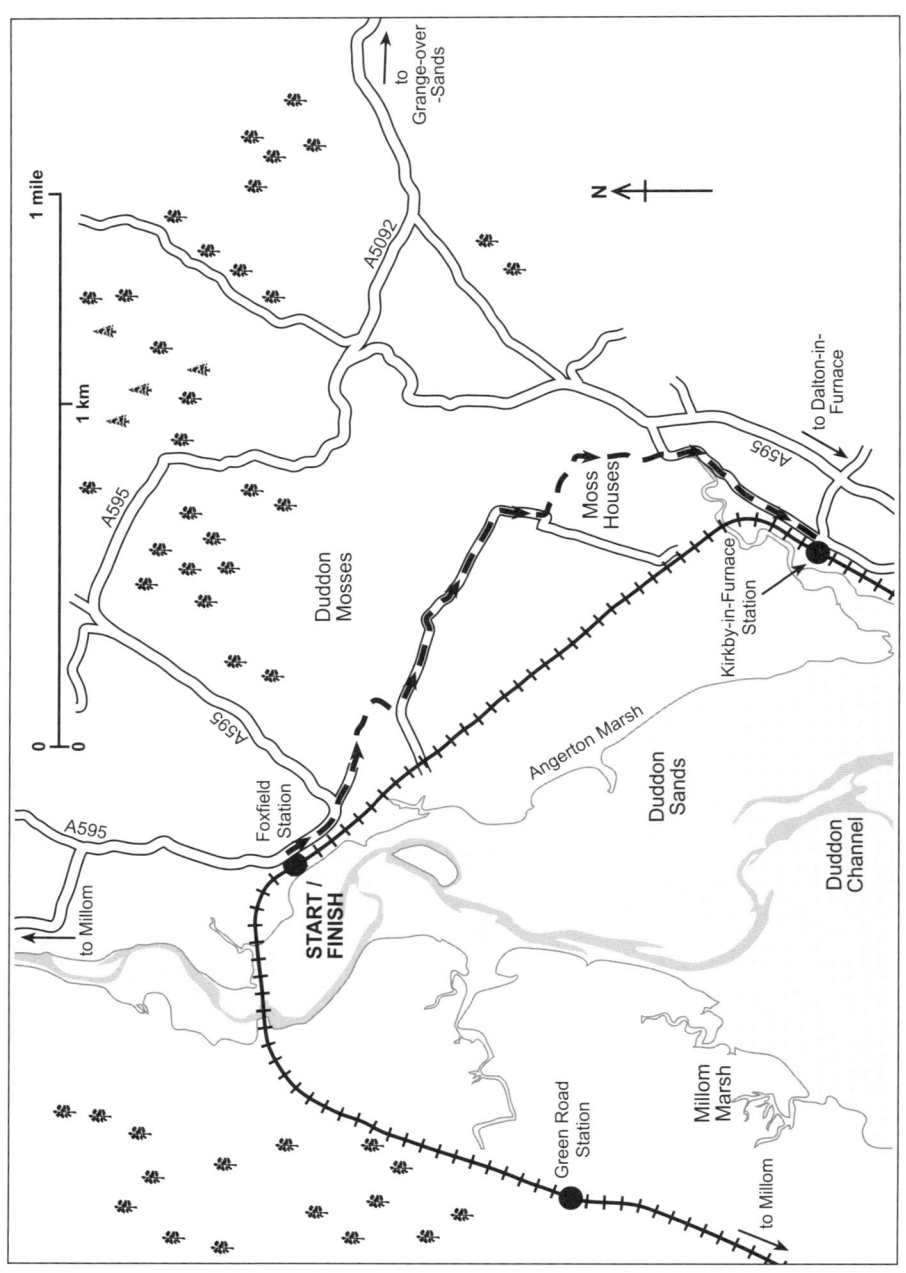

Route

The walk starts from Foxfield Station, which you'll find at grid reference SD 208, 854. Local parking is limited and there is no specific car park, but you should be able to find a spot on one of the local roads.

This walk is, however, better reached by using the train. From the train station, head for the main road, the A595. Take care when crossing from the central platform because this is one of the few stations where you actually have to look both ways and make your way across the tracks.

When you get to the road, turn right onto it and make use of the path on the left. Continue straight ahead on this main road, following as it bends round to the left and passes the level crossing on the right. Around 100m or so further down the road there is another bend to the left and it's here where you take the road off to the right. Follow the footpath sign here to Angerton Moss.

This is a level and well established track, where you should still be on the look-out for cars but it's not very often that one will pop down

The fells gracefully give way to Morecambe Bay in the southern Lakes

here. The road turns into more of a track and just before it bends to the left you should take a path off to the right signed for Duddon Mosses. The path soon bends to the right and eventually brings you out at another track, where you should turn left. As you proceed along here you are passing through the National Nature Reserve; keep to the track and when you pass the farm building at the other side of Duddon Mosses the track becomes a more substantial road.

After a long, straight stretch of road, there is a sharp right hand turn. Continue ahead for around 200m and you'll come to a junction where you turn left. Head beyond the building and continue on the farm track and you'll soon come to a junction of paths at grid reference SD 232, 838. Following the path on the right will take you over a series of fields before bringing you out at local road in Kirkby-in-Furness. Turn right onto it and continue on this road until you reach Sand Side, where you'll find Kirkby-in-Furness Station.

A short train journey back will take you to Foxfield, or you may wish to explore other parts of this fascinating coastline on the train, where you often get the best views as the line runs close to the coast and over a series of coastal viaducts.

Foxfield Station

This quiet and unassuming village is easily overlooked if you're driving around the southern edge of the Lake District, maybe heading towards Wast Water or Ravenglass. But during the 19th century, as the laying of railways opened up many outlying parts of Cumbria, Foxfield started to grow in importance as it became a significant junction.

It was opened in 1848 as the Furness Railway continued the process of expanding its coastal line. The island station was a further stop supporting the local copper industry and the line was extended northwards in the 1850s to give direct access to the mines around Coniston, resulting in a large quantity of raw materials being transported through Foxfield.

Although primarily built for freight transport, the number of passengers using Foxfield did increase in the Victorian era as locals used the trains to get around but also, significantly, as the amount of tourists travelling to this part of the Lakes started to grow. To reflect this, the station needed significant alteration in 1879 as the central platform was widened and a canopy was provided in order to protect passengers from the traditionally wet Cumbrian weather. Tourists

Foxfield Station

were particularly keen to make the trip to Coniston as the link with the Furness Line meant they were able to reach a relatively remote part of the Lake District and connect with the Coniston Steamers at the northern end of the line, which took them out onto the water.

As with many other rural areas, the train service fell victim to the rise of the car. Although Foxfield remains open and still pulls in around 30,000 passengers a year, the tourist element passing through has declined since the branch line to Coniston was closed in 1958. The closure took place long before the Beeching Report had been prepared, meaning that the demise of the railways affected communities in this part of Cumbria years before the axe started to swing elsewhere.

WALK 15
Torver

A section of disused railway track has recently been converted into a footpath and cycle lane, forming the start of a walk which also ventures to the foothills of the Coniston mountain range.

Torver Railway Station

It's possible for you to make Torver's once busy train station a focal point for your Lake District holiday. Whereas it used to welcome freight and passengers, the building has now been converted into two holiday cottages, welcoming tourists who want to stay the week close to Coniston Water.

The original line to Coniston was opened in 1859, with business first arriving at Torver on 18th June. Such was the need for the line up to the area of quarrying around Coniston that it had taken only two years to get fully built following the Act of Parliament that was passed in 1857 to authorise it. Torver itself was used to transport vast quantities of slate and other stone that had been quarried from the surrounding fells.

The Golden Age of Steam was to last just shy of 100 years in this part of the Lake District, with passengers services stopping in October 1958. Four years later the station was also closed to freight and the rail link with the rest of the country was finally severed.

Coniston Water

Although many visitors coming to Coniston today might just fancy a walk by the shore or a trip on the famous steam Gondola, this is a great place for history buffs to learn about the record breaking antics that took place on the water, as well as the tragedy that unfolded in 1967.

Coniston Water has, over the years, been chosen as the place to attempt breaking the water speed record and it was here, in August 1939, that Sir Malcolm Campbell set the record at 141.74 mph in Bluebird K4. His son, Donald, took up the challenge and between 1956 and 1959 he broke the record four times in his Bluebird K7 hydroplane. But other challenges to the record were being made elsewhere and Donald Campbell reckoned he needed to travel at over 300mph to keep the title safe. On 4th January, 1967, he achieved a top speed of over 320 miles an hour but lost control of Bluebird and was killed instantly. The record did not stand as the second leg of the attempt had not been completed. In 2001, the remains of Bluebird and Campbell were recovered from the water. Donald Campbell was buried in the churchyard at Coniston in September, 2001.

Starting point	This lovely Lakeland stroll starts and finishes at the main junction in Torvert - grid reference SD 283, 941
Getting there	Torver sits on the western shores of Coniston Water, and is reached from the north by heading to Ambleside and taking the A593 towards Coniston and then beyond to Torver. From the south, head for the A590 at Greenodd and then take the A5092, turning off towards Torver and Coniston on the A5084. The walk starts at the junction of the A593 and the A5084, with parking available at the junction
Length	4.4km / 2.7 miles
Terrain	1½ hours
Refreshments	On the main road at Torver you will see the large white building that is The Wilson Arms, which offers food drink and a place to stay for those visiting the area. LA21 8BB www.thewilsonsarms.co.uk 01539 441237
Difficulty	Level paths with good accessibility on first section, with a moderate hill climb to follow
Map	OS Explorer OL6 The English Lakes South Western Area
Nearest tourist information	Coniston. Tel: 015394 41533
Next stations	Back in the day when this was a bustling little branch line, Torver's station was sandwiched inbetween Woodland to the south and the terminus of Coniston in the north

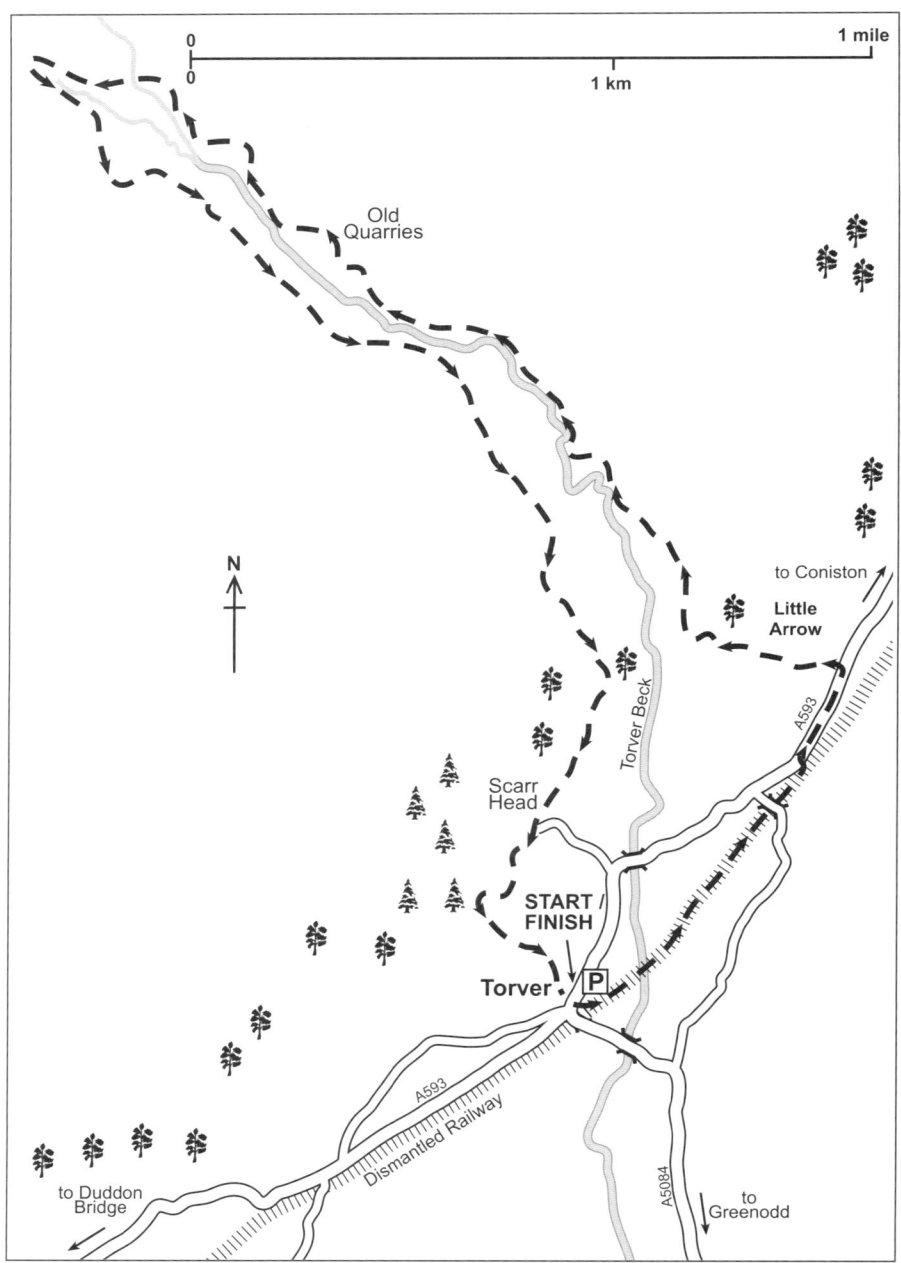

Route

The walk starts at Torver's main junction (SD 283, 941) and it's from here that you need to take the road signed for Lancaster along the A5084. Straight away on the left you need to head along the brand new public bridleway signed for Coniston, recently opened as part of a project to get people walking, cycling and horse riding on the old train route.

You'll soon find yourself on the old railway line, passing the former station on the left. If you glance through the hedge you can make out the edge of the platform, where steam trains destined for Coniston used to pull up. Continue walking along this former railway line, crossing a new wooden bridge that runs directly next to the original railway bridge and crosses over Torver Beck. Go through a gate and proceed along a level section of the walk, ignoring paths off to the left and right and continuing straight on through a couple of gates.

A train worker's shed lays abandoned on the right and just after passing it you'll go under a bridge carrying a local road over the old line. Heading through another couple of gates, you'll soon be brought out at a small settlement called Little Arrow and find yourself on the A593. Turn right and walk on the path which lay at the right side of the road. When you are opposite the cottages on the other side of the road, cross over and take the footpath which cuts through the middle of them. Passing the cottages, you go beyond a cattle grid and over some slate steps in the wall, following the footpath signs as the route bends around to the right and climbs up the hill.

Head on up through a typical lower fell landscape of trees and ferns, turning left as the path takes you through a gate, and then turning off to the right once more. There are clear views of the Coniston Fells in front of you to enjoy now, with the river flowing down to the left and the sound of nearby waterfalls greeting your ears. Head through a gate and cross over a little stream straight after, then more gates await as the path bends down towards the river and turns away from it. The footpath signs will point out where you need to turn left through another gate and head up a small hill where you'll find a wooden marker pointing you straight on, following the river and heading for Walna Scar.

You'll come to ford on the left, which is often too deep to cross, so we'll carry on up a bit. Keep the river on the left and you'll see dramatic fells rising up on the right while huge piles of slate lay straight ahead, highlighting that this was once a very important

The second part of the walk includes a climb up a hill alongside a river quarrying area. When you reach the first pile of slate, walk around it to the left and head for the slate cairn.

Turn left following the bridleway sign, heading through a gate and immediately taking another left. Continue ahead on the track, passing through several gates and heading down this great section of the walk, with walls on either side and some wonderful views in front. Pass a ruined building on the left before reaching the brow of a hill where more views open up. Another ruin is passed on the right before the path heads down to the left and soon brings you into the settlement of Scar Head.

Follow the winding road but after leaving the houses take the path to the right signed for the A593. A couple of stiles on this path and a couple of bends to the left leave you on a path with walls on either side, with the white public house visible ahead of you. Keep this in your sights and you'll soon come out at the Torver junction where you started.

WALK 16
Coniston

From the remains of the platform that once brought Victorian tourists to this classic Lake District village, the walk heads by shops and pubs before heading into the fells towards Levers Water.

Coniston Railway Station

Lancaster architect E. G. Paley was drafted in to design the station building at Coniston for the terminus of the Coniston Branch Line. Opened in 1859, Paley designed the building in the Swiss chalet style, though after closure in 1962 it was abandoned and left to ruin.

Although the sound of whistling steam engines has not been heard in Coniston for some time, let's not forget that at one time this was a busy line for both passengers and freight. So much so, in fact, that the building had to be enlarged between 1888 and 1892 during a refurbishment that cost £4,000. The goods shed and the train shed were later doubled in size and in 1896 a third platform was added.

Route

The car park on Old Furness Road is next to the old Coniston Railway Station and you'll be able to see the platform where Victorian tourists used to get off and begin their Lakeland adventures. There's little other sign that this was a hotbed of railway activity, the area is now the scene of houses and light industry.

With your back to the old station, turn left onto the road and press on until you come to a junction. Turn right here and go down the hill, following it as it bends round to the right. This is Station Road and you should follow it until it brings you out at a cross roads. Turn left and head into the middle of the village, passing a petrol station on the right. Cross over the bridge and follow the road round to the left, passing The Black Bull pub on the left and taking the turn to the left immediately after it.

Follow this country road as it twists and turns out of the village. It will eventually end and turn into a farm track. This is the point when the walk starts to get really wonderful as you leave the village and enter the fells. This farm track starts by heading by some trees, but

Starting point	The car park on Old Furness Road, Coniston. Grid reference SD 299, 974
Getting there	Whether approaching the Lakes from the north or south, a good bet for reaching Coniston is always to head for Ambleside. Once there, take the A593 towards Coniston. At Coniston, head past the petrol station towards Torver and look out for Station Road on the right. Take this and head up until it bends to the left, when you should turn left onto Old Furness Road and look out for the old station on the right
Length	4.8km / 3 miles
Terrain	2¾ hours
Refreshments	There are several pubs to choose from in Coniston village, though my favourite has to the The Black Bull which is the home to Coniston Brewery and serves up a good Cumberland sausage. Tel: 015394 41335 LA21 8DU www.blackbullconiston.co.uk
Difficulty	A challenging walk up to a Lake District tarn
Map	OS Explorer OL6 The English Lakes South Western Area
Nearest tourist information	Coniston. Tel: 015394 41533
Next station	This used to mark the end of the Coniston branch line for the Furness Railway from Foxfields to the south. The first station you would encounter when leaving here was Torver

soon comes out onto the mountain side and you should stick to it as it climbs up, passing a row of old mining cottages on the right.

The track then brings you to a Youth Hostel on the right, but continue beyond it. After this track bends round to the right you will see a river flowing on the left with some brilliant waterfalls crashing down the hill. Continue up, and before you reach the water works building you should take the separate track that turns off up the hill

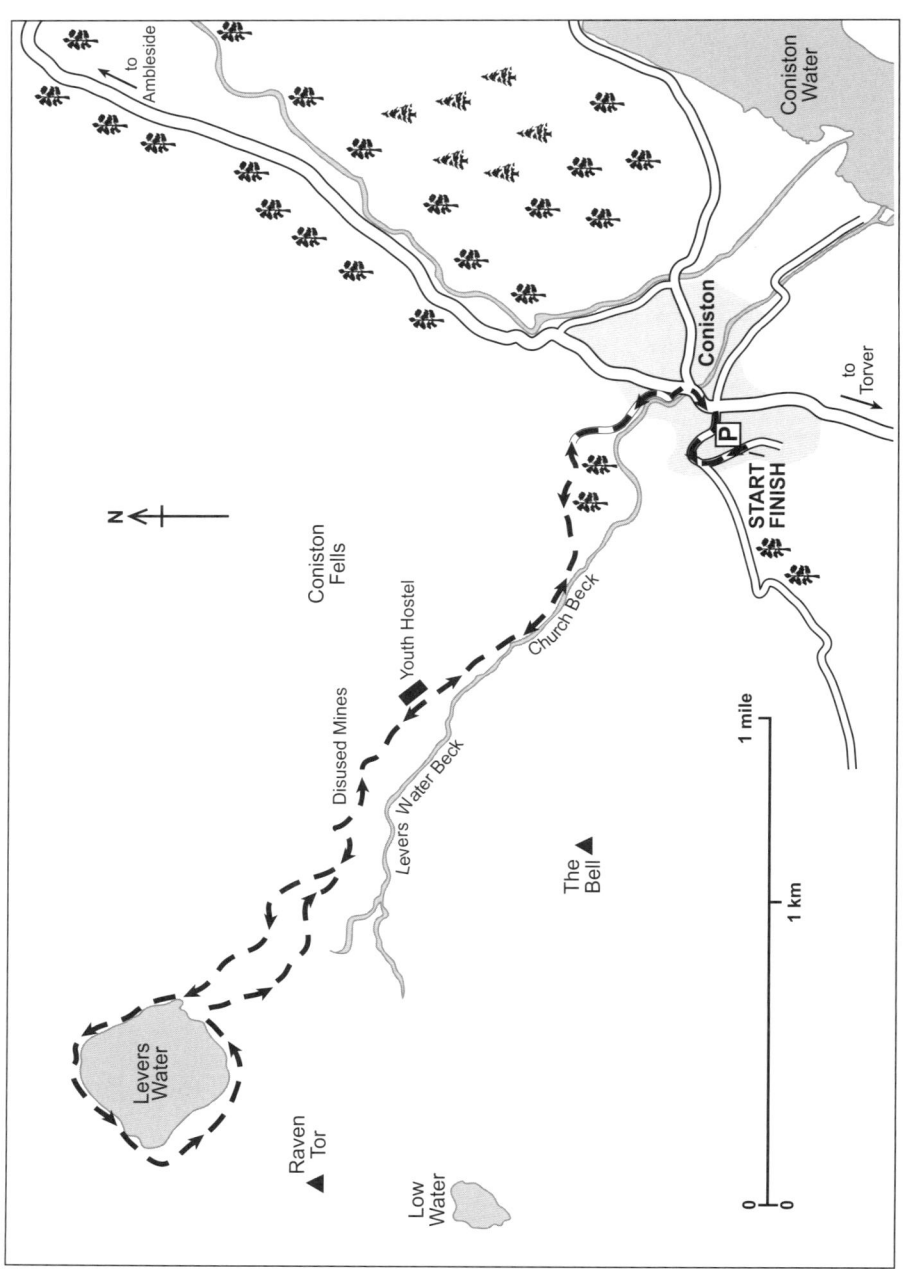

You may well be joined by a few Herdwick Sheep on the way!

to the right. This elevated path gives a view looking down onto the new water treatment building, but also onto lots of old mine workings. Higher up, amazing crags are pretty much everywhere you look.

At the point that the path bends round sharply to the right, you take a path off to the left and cross the river over a wooden footbridge. Once at the other side, take the path off to the right so that you are climbing the hill with the river on your right. This section of the walk is steep and it's tough going, with sections of scree to negotiate and rocks to get over, but some more incredible waterfalls on the right make it worthwhile. The steepness continues, though it levels out briefly as you make your way across a large scree slope. As you continue to climb, you eventually make your way back to the side of the water and will need to climb some rocks to continue on the path.

You'll come to an impressive, tall waterfall with a secondary stream coming around the side of the rock. Continue up on the left hand side of this, where a series of steps will turn into a path. Don't forget to keep checking the view behind you as around here there's a great

Spectacular upland river scenery greets you on the approach to Levers Water

scene all the way down the valley towards Coniston Water.

Once you reach the brow of the hill you can see the dam wall of Levers Water, which was added to turn it into a reservoir. Turn off to the left when you're at the top and start the walk around the water, looking out for a path to the right which will take you down to the edge. The path around the reservoir can be a bit tricky to find and is wet after heavy rain, but it's easy enough to make your way fully around Levers Water. On the final stretch going round the water you pick up a more substantial path, although there will be some boulders for you to negotiate.

When you get back to the dam wall, this time head back down the hill on the other side of the river, keeping the water on your right and following the track. This is a more established track than the one bringing you up, though it can still be dangerous and slippy at times. After a while there is a hairpin bend round to the right and then a bend to the left, which will bring you out at the path you were walking on initially. Follow this down, passing the water building and the Youth Hostel. This track will eventually take you right down to the bottom of the hill, where the track will turn into the country road and this, in turn, will lead you back into Coniston.

Turn right at The Black Bull pub, following the road over the bridge and looking out for Station Road on the right. Take this and follow it up until it brings you out at Old Furness Road, where the walk started.

WALK 17
Keswick

An old train station now used as a hotel marks the starting point for this historic walk along a disused track, the route then looping around Latrigg Fell and gently descending back into Keswick.

Briery Bobbin Mill

Heading out of Keswick on the disused railway you soon come to an abandoned station platform, which is now found close to a caravan park. Until 1958, this was the site of Briery Bobbin Mill, once a bustling cog in the United Kingdom's textile industry that produced an astonishing 40 million bobbins every year – enough to make a line of bobbins 800 miles long!

This part of the Lake District was a key player in bobbin making from the Industrial Revolution and by the 19th century Keswick was at the centre of the world's production. The location for the Briery Bobbin Mill was initially down to the local sources of wood and water, but the coming of the railway was instrumental in the explosion of output and popularity.

Trains were used to bring in wood from all over the world, and take the bobbins back to the market. Ash, beech and birch trees were stacked alongside teak from Burma and boxwood from the Caribbean. Bobbins, of course, were crucial to the textile industry and were the cylinders used to wrap the thread or yarn around. Many different types of bobbins were created at Briery Bobbin Mill for industries all over the world – including the bobbins used to make the coronation robes for Queen Elizabeth II.

The trees around the mill's station were used for the bobbins when poles were cut off them just above the trunk. Subsequent growth of the trees saw several poles shoot up instead of a solitary trunk, and you can still see the evidence for this if you look into the woodland. Once cut, the poles were cut into sections and holes were bored into the middle before they were kiln dried. The top and bottom sections of the bobbin, known as flanges, were then placed onto the bored out pole and the bobbin was complete, ready to be shipped off.

Starting point	The former train station at Keswick, grid reference NY 270, 237
Getting there	Keswick is well sign-posted from the M6 at Junction 40. When you reach the town, follow signs for the Leisure Centre as the disused railway line runs from the hotel close to it. Parking can be an issue and you may have to use nearby car parks and walk to the starting point
Length	8.5km / 5.3 miles
Terrain	3 hours
Refreshments	Several pubs are available in Keswick, but many walks head straight for the Dog and Gun after coming off the fells. From the clock tower in the centre, head towards Lake Road and you'll soon see the white building of the Dog and Gun on the right. Tel: 017687 73463
Difficulty	A fairly steep climb halfway through as you head around Latrigg Fell, though flat at first on the old railway line
Map	OSExplorer OL4 The English Lakes North Western Area
Nearest tourist information	Keswick. Tel: 017687 72645
Next stations	When trains used to arrive in Keswick, travellers had the option of heading east beyond Threlkeld or towards Cockermouth via Braithwaite

Route

As you stand on the former railway station at Keswick, looking at the hotel conservatory that now sits on the platform, your route starts by heading off to the left on the path of the old line. This is a popular route for both walkers and cyclists, forming as it does part of the lovely Coast to Coast path that was championed by famous fell walker Alfred Wainright.

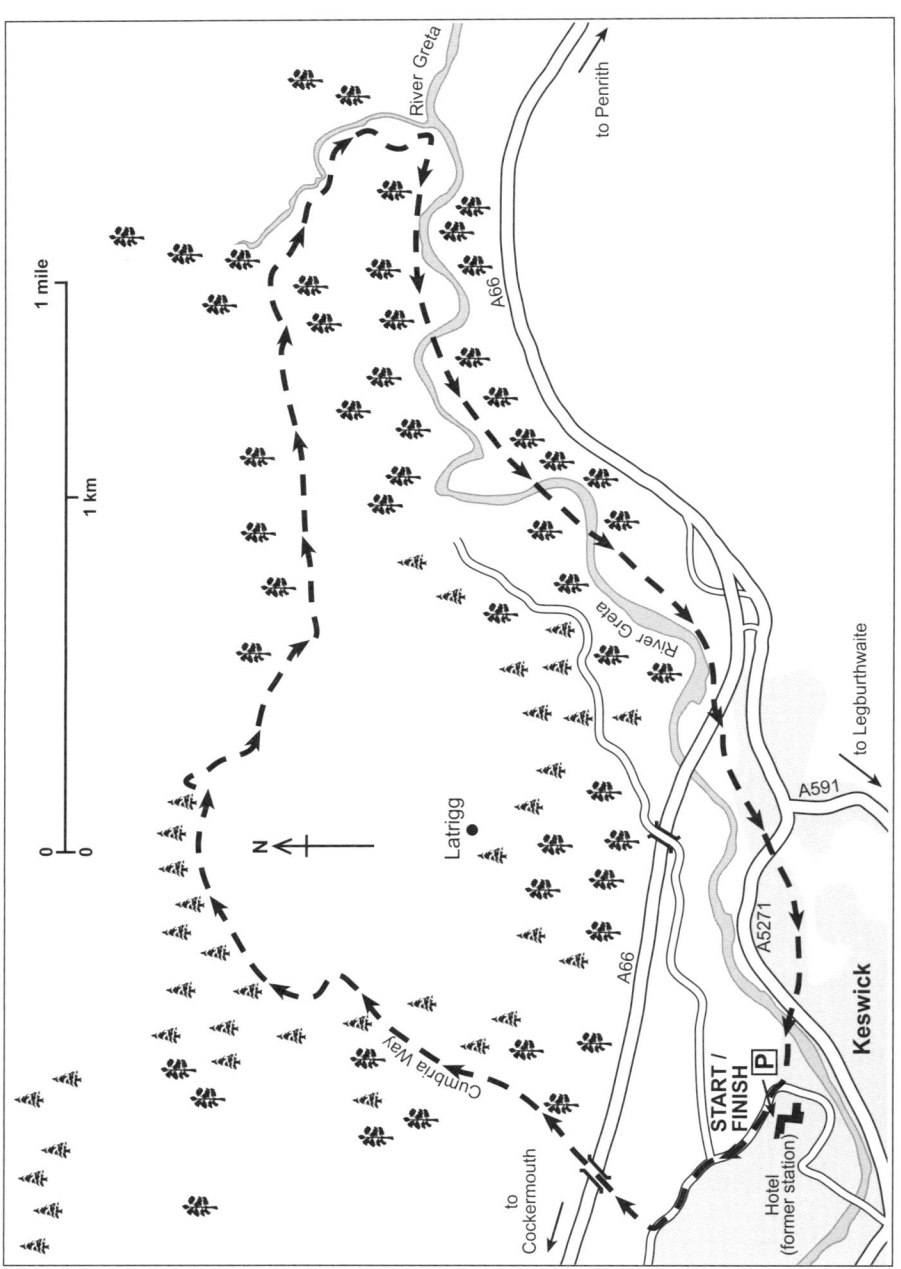

This section of the walk is very easy to follow as you simply need to keep heading straight ahead on the line that once carried steam engines into the northern Lake District. As the former railway line leaves the town of Keswick, it heads over and then under the A5271 before passing under the huge viaduct taking the A66 through the north of the National Park.

At this point, the path is high above the River Greta down to the left and follows a series of wooden paths before picking up more obvious signs of the old railway line. Going past the former site of Briery Bobbin Mill on the left, the line soon opens out a little and you enter an interesting section of the route which features old and rather fantastic looking railway bridges spanning the River Greta. In total you go over three of these, and just before embarking on a fourth crossing you need to keep an eye out on the left for a path (grid reference NY 299, 247).

This is a short path that takes you onto a road, where you need to turn left and climb the hill. Follow the road up before taking a path

Walking where the trains once ran, this walk takes you over some historically important railway bridges

111

The route back to Keswick is an opportunity to get an elevated view of the northern Lake District

off to the left at the top, heading through a gate and following a track that keeps a small wood on the right. Soon after, there'll be an option to take a path on the left that climbs up the grassy bank, but you need to head straight on along the track, bending round to the left and once again keeping woodland on your right.

As you head further on, the path will get closer to the woodland and eventually this route will lead you up to a road, where you will find a car park (NY 280, 253). Head straight ahead on the road but after a short time you will see a path off to the left. This is the Cumbria Way, a popular long distance path that will be your route down the hill and back into Keswick. Ignore all paths leading off this route and continue to wind your way through the woods and once again down into the town.

As the track nears the bottom of the fell, it will take you over the A66 and shortly after you'll reach a T-junction, where you should turn left. Following this road, which still makes up part of the Cumbria Way, will bring you back to the Keswick Leisure Centre and the area around the hotel where the walk started.

WALK 18
Bassenthwaite Lake

Explore the forest trails of the northern Lake District and enjoy the views of Bassenthwaite Lake and Derwent Water.

Bassenthwaite Lake Railway Station

You're likely to have travelled along the route of the disused railway in order to reach the starting point for the walk as some of it is now covered by the A66. Most people whizz by without the slightest idea that this was indeed a stopping point for tourists wanting to stroll by the lake, as well as a regular form of transport for the villagers of Dubwath. Indeed, the house that is visible from the road and is still used as a home today used to be the station master's house.

Close by to that, and obscured by trees that have grown up around it, is the old station building. Now roofless and looking a little sorry for itself, it's a reminder that engines used to chug by here from Penrith en route to Cockermouth.

The scene of yesteryear; tourists once flocked to this lake by steam train before cars were commonplace *(photograph: Ben Brooksbank)*

Bassenthwaite Lake Station opened on 2nd January, 1865 and survived for just over 100 years before being closed down in the Beeching Report, carrying the last passengers in April 1966. Much of the Penrith to Cockermouth line to the west of Keswick became the A66 road we know today in what is a very symbolic transformation from the Age of Steam to the domination of the car. But the line to the east of Keswick had a reprieve and continue to shuttle passengers into the Lake District into the 1970s. Sadly, it too has now closed – although local plans to reopen the line are gaining momentum.

Starting point	Parking on the road near the Station House, located off the A66 at the north of Bassenthwaite Lake. Grid reference: NY 198, 309
Getting there	From the M6 take Junction 40 and head along the A66 towards Keswick. Continue on the A66 beyond the town and look out for the old station house on the left, close to Dubwath. Take the turning for the Pheasant Inn and park on the road
Length	9.8km/ 6.1 miles
Terrain	3 hours
Refreshments	The Pheasant Inn is signed off the main A66 road and is about a quarter of a mile from the start of the walk, well worth stopping off at. Tel: 01768 776234 CA13 9YE www.the-pheasant.co.uk
Difficulty	A challenging walk around woodland in the northern lakes
Map	OSExplorer OL4 The English Lakes North Western Area
Nearest tourist information	Keswick. Tel: 017687 75738
Next stations	Now disused, this station used to be the stop between Embleton and Braithwaite

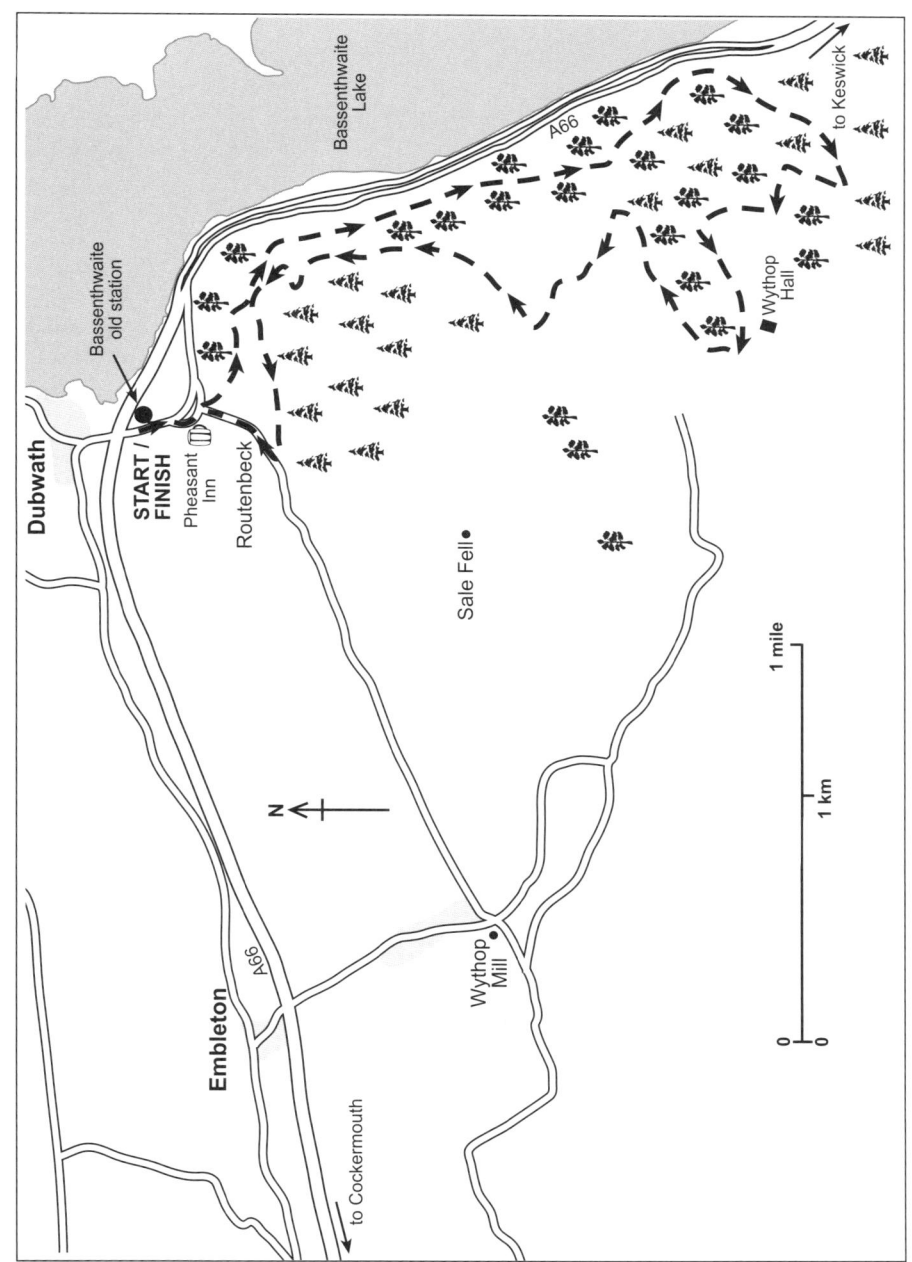

Route

From the A66 on the west side of Keswick there is a sign off to the Pheasant Inn. You can park anywhere around this quiet road, and many walkers do, but the old station can been seen on the western side of this looping road. From here, walk towards the Pheasant Inn, turning off to the right and passing the pub on the left.

Take the road that goes by the side of the pub, signed for Wythop Mill, and shortly after passing the pub you'll see a footpath sign on the left. Enter here and pick up a path that heads up into the woods. As you climb, you'll have a fence on the right and several fallen trees on the left. The path bends to the left as it climbs, bringing you to an opening where you turn right onto a track. Look out for a path on the left and this one will take you up to another track, where you turn left and double back on your previous direction. You'll soon see some buildings down to the left and shortly after take the path that leads up the hill to the right.

As you reach the brow, the path bends to the right and you can see Bassenthwaite Lake on the left. Continue on here, ignoring the path up to the right and taking care to mind the steep drop to the left. This is an easy track to follow, with great views of the lake and the Skiddaw range beyond it. Look out for a path off to the right (grid reference NY 208, 281) marked by a wooden pole and yellow arrow. This takes you into the woods, cross over a track and head up as the path bends around and soon takes you up a steep section on tree roots which double as steps. You come out onto a clearing and should follow the marker across the opening, going over a stile and into deciduous woodland, with a distinctly different feel to the pine-dominated areas.

This part of the wood is occasionally used for archery and you'll see a warning sign as you enter and also targets up the hill on the right. Look out for the farmland on the left as the path continues through the wood, passing more archery targets. The path bends around the left through Hogg Park, with Wythop Hall down to the left. An incredible and surprising view opens up ahead of you as the path bends to the right. Go through a gate and continue on the path, keeping the fence on your left and following it as it edges round to the right.

Sale Fell lies up to the left. Cross over a stile and keep going in the same direction, with the fence now on your right. Go over a couple more stiles and follow the path as it bends to the left and, when it comes to a larger track, turn left again onto Cycle Route 71. There's a good view of Ling Fell from here, and as the Cycle Route turns off to the left your journey takes you straight ahead. This takes you by the buildings at Lothwaite Side and soon you'll come to another track, where you should turn right.

This section of the walk has the best views, off to the right being the Skiddaw Range, Bassenthwaite Lake and also Derwent Water. You then enter the wood again and continue along the track, the majority of this section heading downhill, fairly steeply in places. You'll come to a clearing with a track going up to the right, but make sure you take the path down ahead to the left here, continuing down over a stream and down further until you come out at a road in the village of Routenbeck. Turning right here will take you back to the Pheasant Inn, where a couple of left turns on the local roads will bring you back out to the starting point.

You'll be able to see Bassenthwaite Lake and Derwent Water after climbing up through the woods.

WALK 19
Threlkeld

Walk along the former railway track in the northern Lake District before taking a path by the river in a short circular stroll passing some of Cumbria's industrial heritage.

The Cockermouth, Keswick and Penrith Railway

There's the still the central platform standing at the former Threlkeld Railway Station, now much covered in moss and surrounded by trees that have shot up since the line closed for good in 1972. But the demise of this line that once brought thousands of visitors into the northern Lake District was a staggered one, all dating back to 1963 when Dr Beeching published his infamous report and recommended that trains stop passing through the likes of Keswick, Threlkeld and Bassenthwaite. And so, in 1966 all the passenger services west of Keswick were withdrawn and much of the route was eventually replaced by the planned A66 road when it was finally opened in 1977.

The service between Keswick and Penrith, including those stopping at Threlkeld, managed to cling on. But not for long, as the writing was already daubed on the station wall. The last service to carry people to and from Threlkeld and Keswick was in 1972.

The demise of the railway in this part of Cumbria was a sorry one when compared to the excitement at setting it up in the 19th century. Back in 1861 there was a station at Penrith on the West Coast Mainline as well as one at Cockermouth on the Cockermouth and Workington Railway. An Act of Parliament was passed that approved the linking of these two towns, meaning a new 31.5 mile track was to be constructed and stations built at eight places inbetween. The line opened in 1865 and many artefacts from the Victorian era can be seen on display at Keswick Museum and Art Gallery, including tickets from the 1th century, a platform guard's whistle and even the spade used to cut the first earth for the railway to be laid in 1862.

Route

From the car park, head onto the disused railway line and turn right onto it, heading away from Keswick and passing a row of old station

What are ewe staring at?

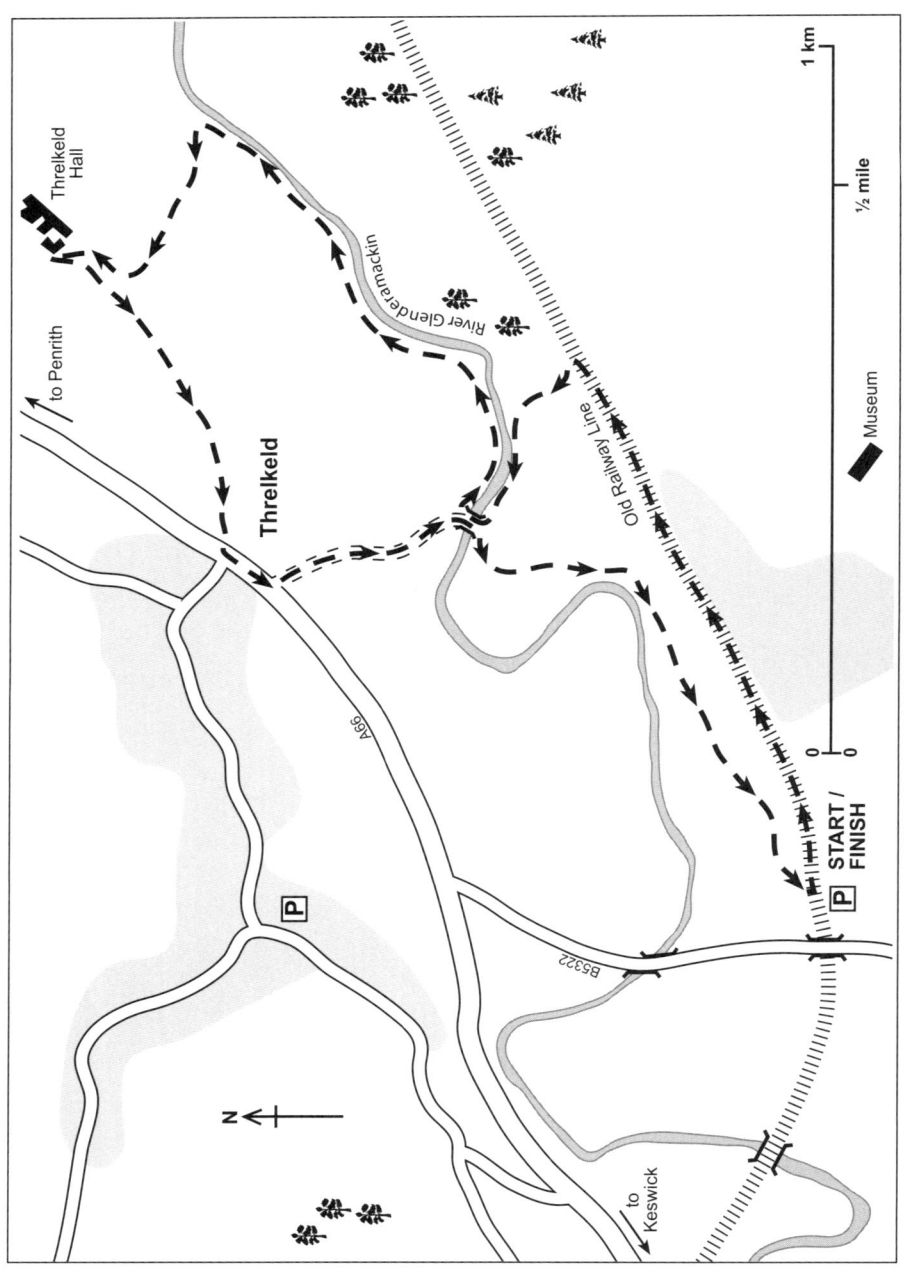

Starting point	Take the B5322 from the A66 near Threlkeld. The car park near Townfield Bridge at grid reference NY 320, 245.
Getting there	Threlkeld is nice and easy to find on the right side of the A66 as you head from Penrith to Keswick. It's well signed and you need to leave the M6 and Junction 40 in order to find it. The former railway station is at the other side of the A66 to the village, following the brown sign for the museum
Length	3.9km/2.2 miles
Terrain	1 hour
Refreshments	The Horse and Farrier has been in Threlkeld for over 300 years and it's an ideal place to enjoy a drink and a bite to eat after the walk. Tel: 017687 79688 CA12 4SQ www.horseandfarrier.com
Difficulty	Much of it on the level, with some steep slopes encountered, all on established paths
Map	OSExplorer OL4 The English Lakes North Western Area
Nearest tourist information	Keswick. Tel: 017687 72645
	Keswick would have been the next station stop heading west towards Cockermouth, with Troutbeck being the next chance to alight on the way to Penrith

cottages on the right. Go through a gate and you can see Threlkeld away to the left, with a large wall on the right. Go through another gate and walk onwards until you approach an old bridge that the trains used to steam underneath, but you don't go under this as the public access to the old line ends here.

Turn left on the path, then, and turn left once more when you reach the road, heading down the hill. As you get down to the River Glenderamackin it bends round to the left. You'll soon come to Mill

Bridge. Cross it and follow the path on the right next to the river. This continues following the course of the river until you come to a small road; off to the right you'll see the gold course, but you should turn left.

This footpath winds its way up towards Threlkeld Hall though a caravan site. When you reach the hall, look out for a gate on the left signalling the start of a footpath that will take you straight ahead at first and then bending round to the right towards the A66. When you reach the main road there is a very short section on a path to the left before you take the first left signed for Bridge End. At the end of the track, cross the bridge and take the path off to the right signed for Townfield Bridge.

Stick to this path and the fence on the left as it takes you across fields and over a stream with a stone bridge, at this point branching off to the right. Go through a gate and turn right onto another path, which takes you over by a stream and through a narrow gap in a wall.

Continue ahead, passing the farm and the campsite, and stick to the path until it brings you out at Townfield Bridge, where you can see the remains of the railway bridge once carrying trains to Keswick. Turn left at the road and the first left after the bridge to reach the car park.

WALK 20
Oxenholme

On the eastern fringes of the National Park, this trail leaves from a trail station but soon takes up the route of a canal that is no more.

Oxenholme Lake District Station

For such a small settlement, it's quite amazing that Oxenholme has its own mainline train station. It's certainly the only village on the West Coast line where trains bound for London, Manchester, Glasgow and Edinburgh stop off. The reason, of course, is the Lake District and the majestically rising skyline of mountains visible from the comfy seats in the north and south-bound carriages. To this end, the official name of this station is Oxenholme Lake District although it's quite often and very reasonably shortened to Oxenholme by locals and visitors alike. Oxenholme is, of course, the station that links the West Coast Main Line to the Lake District, via the Windermere branch that calls in at Kendal, Staveley and Burneside.

Oxenholme has been a bustling station since the line to Scotland was created *(photograph: Ben Brooksbank)*

Walks from those other stations are also featured in this book and although the line to Windermere gradually gets further and further into the National Park, this walk from Oxenholme, just outside the border, takes in some great countryside. And it's not just about railway heritage here either; part of the walk takes on the former route of the Lancaster Canal, which is a route you may want to investigate in more depth.

As you might expect for a train station giving access to one of the country's most scenic areas, Oxenholme is well utilised. Just under half a million passengers use the station every year and the village is remarkably well served when you consider its size.

The station at Oxenholme was opened in 1847, when it was known as Kendal Junction. By the 1860s it had been renamed Oxenholme, a name that suited it well until relatively recently. The decision to rebrand the station as Oxenholme Lake District was taken in 1988 and

Starting point	Oxenholme train station at grid reference SD 531, 901
Getting there	Oxenholme is on the main West Coast Mainline and by road take Junction 36 from the M6 and follow signs for Kendal and Oxenholme
Length	9.2km / 5.7 miles
Allow	3 hours
Refreshments	Conveniently located and with a railway history, The Station Inn is a good place to visit. Tel: 01539 724094 LA9 7RF www.stationinnoxenholme.co.uk
Difficulty	A straightforward stroll, with some country roads and the option of spending longer in Kendal
Map	OS Explorer OL7 The English Lakes South Eastern Area
Nearest tourist information	Kendal. Tel: 01539 735891
Next stations	Next stop heading towards the Lakes is Kendal, while on the West Coast Main Line Oxenholme is sandwiched between Lancaster and Penrith

By rivers, roads, railways and the route of former canals; this route takes in a cross section of features in the eastern lakes

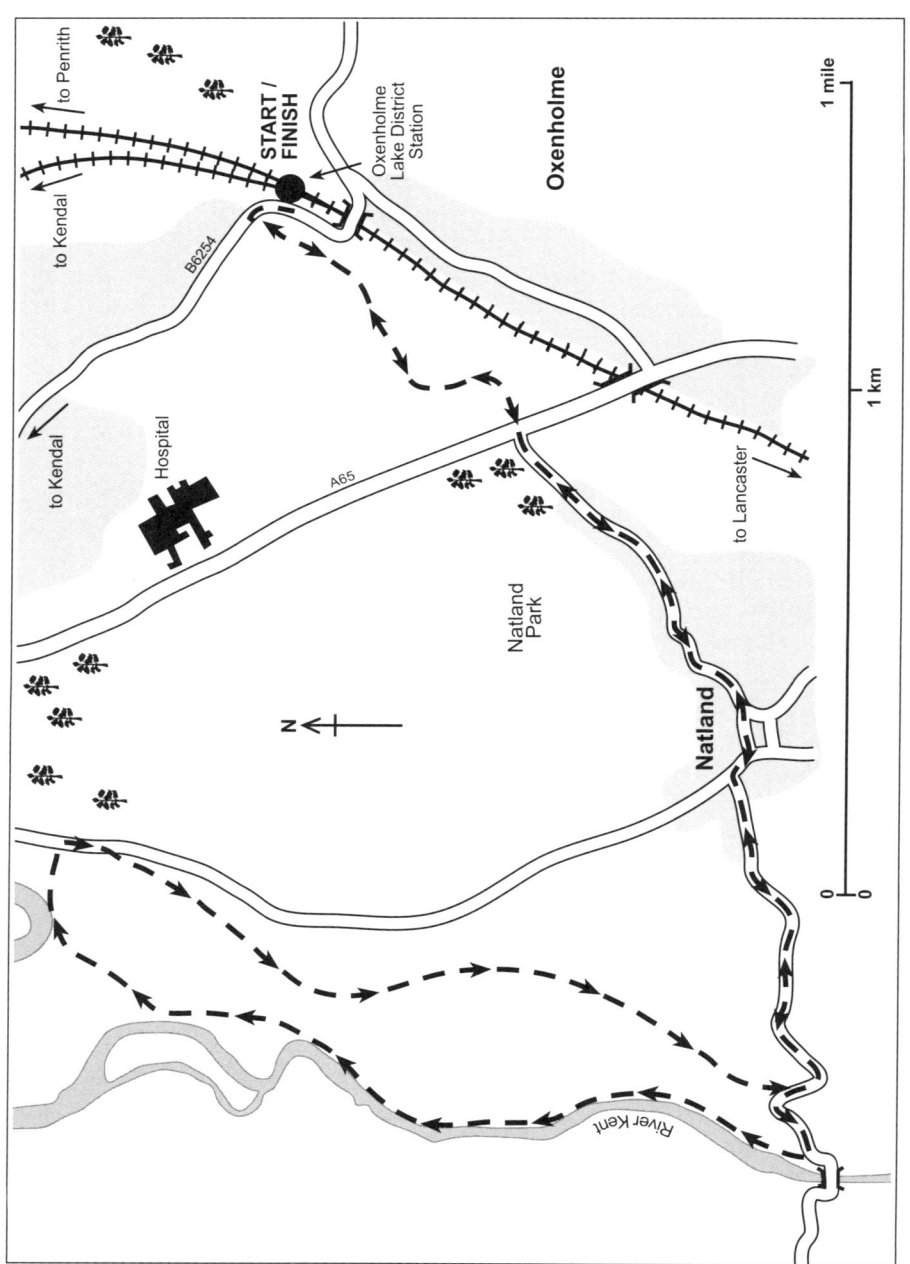

left travellers in no doubt where they should get off to catch their connection to Windermere.

If you've read the *Swallows and Amazons* series of books you may be familiar with the Strickland Junction station, which author Arthur Ransome based on Oxenholme.

Route

Leave the train station via the car park entrance and turn right onto Oxenholme Road. The road will bend around to the left and you'll soon see a footpath off to the left, which you need to take. This is a straightforward path to follow, which has the train line on the left and you'll probably see a high speed train or two while on the way.

The path heads through farming fields and soon bends its way around Brow Head Farm before coming out at the A65. Carefully cross the road and take the country road opposite down the towards the village of Natland along Oxenholme Lane. As you enter Natland, keep on Oxenholme Lane and work your way towards the centre, passing the village green and soon after branching off to the right and going on Natland Road. Take the first left off here, though, down Hawes Lane until you reach Hawes Bridge, where you will find your path signed to Kendal off to the right on the nearside of the river.

You will immediately enter a small area of woodland and as you press on you'll go through a gap in the wall to enter farmland. Cross fields using gates and stiles, keeping the river close on your left until it bends off to the left and your path goes straight ahead. Keep left of the grassy hill in front of you and then head right toward Natland Road when you get to the path. At the road, turn right and keep on the pavement at the side of the road for a short while, until you see a footpath off to the right pointing you along the Lancaster Canal Trust trail, now heading towards Tewitfield. The path is fenced in, and you'll soon see links to another form of transport.

You may be more used to seeing railway heritage on the walks in this book, but there are signs that you are walking by what used to be an old canal. Cross a couple of stiles before seeing a rather unusual vision; an old canal bridge in the middle of a field because the canal itself has since been filled in. Continue along the embankment and head for the gate at the end of the field, turning left onto it and walking into Natland once more.

Turn right at the end of the road and head into the village, passing the village green on the right and sticking to the road on the left towards Oxenholme. When you reach the main road, cross over and take the path into the field next to the bus stop. Follow this all the way across the fields until you come out at another road. Turn right and you'll find yourself at the station.